Spring Returning

a selection from the works of
James Farrar

made and introduced by
Christopher Palmer

Autolycus Press

Is it too grim a burden, to maintain
A will, that murder shall not rule again?
That bloody man shall cage, like bloody beast?
Man must not make less beauty than the flower.
Youth, given back from slaughter, has an hour.
Lighten us, life: shine, planet, in our east.

– JOHN MASEFIELD, Poet Laureate
(printed in *The Times* on
VE Day, May 8 1945)

1986   Christopher Palmer
Farrar extracts © RAF Benevolent Fund
Book design © 1986 Autolycus Press

This book shall not be reproduced, either in part or in whole, without the written permission of the publishers, Autolycus Press, 14 Barlby Road, London W10 6AR.

ISBN 0 903413 76 0

Printed in England by The Wembley Press, Reading, Berkshire.

Contents

The publishers wish to thank the Henry Williamson Literary Estate, who have waived their royalty on this publication, proceeds from which will go to the RAF Benevolent Fund. The editor gratefully acknowledges the help and encouragement he has received from the late Margaret Farrar, David and Bridget Farrar, Michael Horsman, Gilbert Wild, Alwyn Trubshaw, Anne Williamson, Frances Palmes, Daphne Odin-Pearce, and members of the Henry Williamson Society. Their devoted co-operation has made this new edition possible.

*   *   *   *   *

The Henry Williamson Society can be contacted through the secretary: Mary Heath, Longclose, Langtree, Torrington, North Devon.

Introduction

I'm starting to write this essay on the 40th anniversary of V.E. Day.
On 8 May 1945 the war in Europe officially ended. The civilisation
that had been raised in Europe on the double foundation of classical
thought and the Christian faith and thence propagated round the world,
centred on the inalienable rights and dignity of the individual; the work
of centuries of advance, in which humanity had been aspiring towards
finer forms of political and spiritual living: these were what the Nazi
despotism had systematically set out to destroy. As Thomas Mann
would have said, it wanted to *un*-write the Ninth Symphony. It came
perilously close to succeeding. That it did not was due to the courage
and determination of millions of fighting men and women, countless
numbers of whom did not survive to see victory assured. These were
foremost in the mind of King George VI when, at 9pm on 8 May, he
broadcast a message to the nation in which he said: 'We have come
to the end of our tribulation; and they are not with us at the moment
of our rejoicing.' One of them was a young airman-poet called James
Farrar, the author of this book, a writer not merely of great promise,
but also of partial fulfilment. He was discovered, for the world at large,
posthumously, by Henry Williamson. After Farrar died, his mother
Margaret – who already had more than an inkling of her son's unusual
talent – submitted some of his verses, essays and prose-poems to a
well-known literary magazine of the time called *The Adelphi*, edited by
John Middleton Murry. (She had laboriously taught herself to type rather
than entrust the precious manuscript to a disinterested professional
typist.) Murry told Williamson that he had accepted them almost
before he finished reading them. At once he had felt the 'indefinable
shock of reality' in the pages. Williamson, reading them, must have
felt more than that. He must have realised, immediately, intuitively,
that he himself had been, unwittingly, the spiritual mentor of the young
writer who, he now learned to his abiding sorrow, had died in battle
nearly two years before – in July 1944. The two had never met; yet
the elder knew in the younger one of his company of 'friends in ancient
sunlight'. For Williamson 'a sense of [Farrar's] potential as a great
writer, in some way that can only be described as mystical, remains,

despite his physical disappearance (the dead are often with the living).'[1] Williamson wrote to Mrs Farrar from Georgetown in Devon:

> I think that the poems and prose of your son are very fine, and I would much care to help put them into permanent form − a book ... I think James was one of the true voices of the late war. If the idea appeals to you will you please write to me ... I do not feel that James is really dead: the lore of the spirit does not fade with the body. (13 July 1947)

About two years later, a member of the London publishing firm of Williams & Norgate looked out of his office window and saw Henry Williamson walking up Great Russell Street with what was obviously a great pile of manuscripts. He ran down and introduced himself, whereupon Williamson explained that he was on his way to another publisher with the literary remains of a Mosquito navigator who had been killed over the Channel at the age of twenty, while attempting to destroy a flying-bomb. The upshot of this chance street-encounter was an offer on the part of Williams & Norgate to publish *The Unreturning Spring* (the title, after a poem by Laurence Binyon, was chosen by Margaret Farrar) and the book duly appeared in 1950. It created a sensation in the press. I quote from a selection of the reviews:

> ... the letters, essays, stories and journal reveal a prose-mastery that at any age would be remarkable and at 15−20 is amazing ... behind every word is the questing, aspiring, probing soul of the poet. (C A Renshaw, *Sheffield Telegraph*, 26 January 1951)

> ... for better or for worse the life of the airfield is a new experience for man, and James Farrar is its youthful laureate. High talent he had for words, but the genius lay in that inner control which acted upon the ardour and aspirations of youth like the judgement of maturity. (*The Times*, 23 March 1951)

John Pudney wrote: 'This, it seems to me, is a very real and living memorial to all that was most sensitive, civilised, creative and mature which perished in the war.' Richard Aldington: 'There's a flash when he puts the fact down'; and Air Marshal Sir Richard Peck: '... it was interesting to see that a young man with a fine mind, so sensitive to

---

[1] *The Adelphi*, October − December 1948, p. 10. Editorial by Henry Williamson entitled (after Middleton Murry) 'The Lost Legions'.

impressions and to the beauty of nature, should excel also in the performance of his service duties.' And so on.

Williamson himself had contributed a valuable introduction to the miscellany which he slightly expanded when, in 1968, Chatto & Windus re-issued *The Unreturning Spring*. Kenneth Allsop's view then was that, for those who had fought in the war, its authenticity of atmosphere and log-book factual accuracy 'will instantly impale the survivors' (of which he was one). 'Even those immune to nostalgia for that bleakly traumatic interlude, when their schoolboy selves were undergoing crash-course conversion into technical killers, will acknowledge instant recognition ... one constantly recalls with astonishment that Farrar was still not 21 when he died, for he was a natural. The creative gift was powerful in him, an inner clarity and quality, an authority of imaginative expression far beyond his actual experience' (*Spectator*, 17 January 1969). And Richard Church, in *Country Life* (12 December 1968), praised the objective readability of the prose: '(Farrar) must have been born a professional: that is, a craftsman more interested in his job than in himself.' He summed up: 'With Sidney Keyes and Keith Douglas, two other poets lost in the Second World War, he leaves a springtime gathering of his own words, and their fragrance has survived' – unwittingly rehearsing an image employed by Henry Williamson when he wrote to Mrs Farrar: 'Yes, I do understand what you live for and by, and how your thoughts are ever of that blue flower of your life that is still in bloom, and will remain so.'

James Farrar, or Jim (as everyone called him, and as I shall from now on), was born 5 October 1923 at Woodford in Essex, the second son of a father who had served in the Royal Flying Corps and had crashed badly.* His elder brother, David (who appears occasionally in Jim's journal and letters), became a distinguished engineer; he is at present Director of the Centre of Engineering Design at Cranfield Institute of Technology.

The parents separated when the boys were still young, and their mother brought them up. Jim went to school in Sutton, in Surrey, which was then becoming part of Greater London. Originally he planned to enter the Civil Service; but the outbreak of war caused the Entrance

---

* Cf. one of Jim's letters to his mother, 4 May 1943 '... for myself I get a hell of a kick out of (flying). I suppose it's the family air-mindedness that stands me in good stead.'

Examination to be suspended, and he went for some months to work on a farm in Manaccan, in Cornwall (this was a time, of course, when many London children were evacuated to the provinces for fear of bomb attacks on the capital). He loved farm life and the countryside, became adept both at milking cows and at lying on his back gazing into the sun, generally somewhere like the Dennis Head or St. Anthony, where he had a view of the sea. All the time he was making what he called 'recordings on the soundtrack of memory' and it was now that he began to keep a large note-book and to copy into it poems, prose-sketches, short stories, random reflections and observations – anything which came into his mind. Curiously, his farming friends saw no sign of these literary activities; rather were they impressed above all by his sketching, and thought he would eventually become an artist. They also noted an unusually high level of conversation, more like that of a grown man than of a sixteen-year-old boy.[1]

Early in 1940, the 'phoney war' period, he returned to London to work in an accountant's office – a death-sentence, he called it: 'Bilious winter afternoon in the office. Sitting in the de-oxygenated atmosphere known as comfort. Feet vaguely chilly, hands like portions of fish straight from slab. Brain shuttered down to one-fifth aperture.'[2] A poem on London's morning rush-hour recalls Eliot: –

> This is a river of black and brown,
> Slugged, too, its slouching paces,
> Lit like the water sinking down –
> Beaded with misty-sunlit, sunless faces.

This would not do for Jim. At seventeen-and-a-half he volunteered for the RAF and he was called up soon after his eighteenth birthday. Thereafter his writings tell his own story – until the pre-dawn hours of 26 July 1944, when a Mosquito aircraft on patrol over the approaches to the Thames and London was ordered to intercept and destroy an incoming VI flying bomb. Radar at Operational Headquarters showed

---

[1] He returned to Cornwall in 1944 to spend his last leave. Walter Eva, owner of the farm on which Jim stayed both then and before, found he had grown into 'a tall, rather handsome officer with a beautiful flow of English. His shyness had disappeared, but he still seemed far away in his thoughts. He had spent four of his seven days' leave when D-Day came and he packed immediately, saying that he must return as his squadron would want him.' (*The Cornishman*, 24 July 1952).

[2] *The Unreturning Spring* (henceforward *US*), p. 45.

attacker and target close, merge and then suddenly disappear from the screen. (Presumably the aircraft went in too close to the attack of the VI, but no-one knows for certain what happened). That morning Mrs. Farrar received her last letter from Jim, dated two days earlier, typically full of concern for Fred Kemp, his pilot, whose house had been shattered by a flying bomb a few days before, but who'd managed to evacuate his wife and children to Swansea. He ended: 'I hope to God I have a peacetime for *my* children. Well, that's all for now. Love, Jim.' Fred's body was eventually recovered from the Channel; Jim's never was. 'We live by death's negligence,' he'd written in his notebook. 'Perhaps a tenth of my generation will be a part of foreign earth, or dumb things that the tides push.'

For all his youth and inexperience, Jim seems to have made a lasting impression on all who knew him. He had an immensely attractive, even charismatic, personality. Henry Williamson described him as 'a happy youth with a great appetite for life. He was a good boy, in the true sense of the word. He was keen, he worked hard, he strove for truth, he kept himself fit for his work, he lived in a sense of his own humility, he never set himself up to be better than his fellows ... He was in this like the famous man akin to him in quality and perception, Aircraftman "T.E. Shaw" (Lawrence of Arabia).'[1] Jim's brother David appended a physical description:[2]

> Jim was tall (about six foot two inches) and broad-shouldered. He was naturally of spare build, largely owing to tuberculosis when he was about seven years old: but his recovery was complete, and when in the R.A.F. he was strong and becoming well developed. His complexion was fresh, his hair brown and wavy, his eyes blue-grey. Normally he was clear and serious in manner, and he had a wonderful knack of making people (no matter who they were) feel at ease with him, even after only a minute's acquaintance: but his sense of humour was lively and was often expressed in mime. Always informal, he would invariably get into an old sports coat and flannels when on leave, although his uniform was always kept immaculate when he was back at his station.

We don't need to read very far in Jim's writing to become aware of the zest and relish for life which so engaged Williamson. Even the devil-darkness of war cast few shadows on a world he perceived as

---

[1] Introduction to *US*, p. 10.
[2] Ibid., pp. 10–11.

indescribably lovely: 'The wonder of the earth to be captured, the green song of summer, the cadence of seasons'.[1] He had an infinite capacity for enjoyment — 'I feel like thanking whatever was responsible for my creation for my ability to draw real entertainment from the ordinary.'[2] 'Happiness comes to me in the strangest ways, seldom if ever predicted. It can come in a printed word, a glance, a colour or scent, a voice, any ordinary thing which suddenly shines with significance.'[3] People in particular fascinated him: 'Whoever they are, whether I like them or not, whether they like me or not, they are of unending interest. I think if you try to develop observation, boredom is cut down to almost nothing in any circumstances.'[4] 'I wouldn't have known the first thing about life but for this marvellous series of ephemeral companionships and relationships'.[5] Whatever task was Jim's he worked with a will. His mother in later years claimed that she felt no bitterness about his early death in action,[6] 'because he was doing what he wanted to do'. We cannot but wonder at the ease and effortlessness with which he so early shaped his life into harmony and balance and meaning. His religious views and general philosophy of life are expounded in his writing with great commonsense clarity and conviction. Details of his really private life — his emotional and sexual development — are not confided to his journal or diary, but we can be sure that he was as well-integrated and well-rounded a personality in these respects as in all the others.[7]

But perhaps we should temper our astonishment. Jim was a poet, and like all poets,

> Farrar could write anything he saw; and he'd get it right. He saw it with delight, with great interest, with understanding; and he could penetrate ... He had the *divining* mind; and the divining mind is the God-like mind.[8]

---

[1] *US*, p. 56.
[2] Ibid, p. 115.
[3] Ibid, p. 82.
[4] Ibid, p. 78.
[5] Ibid., p. 196.
[6] The wording of her 'In Memoriam' notice suggests as much: 'Remembering with love and a tender pride my happy warrior who flew "beyond the light of the last star" on the night of July 25/26, 1944 — M.'
[7] The occasional references to 'Waafery' and 'popsying' tend to be rather perfunctory and juvenile, and there is no suggestion that his various encounters and affairs with girls ever counted for much in his life. In fact the only person outside his family for whom Jim seems to have felt a strong and deep attachment was his boyhood friend Don Powell, who inspired one of his tenderest pieces of poetic prose (see pp. 43–4).
[8] Henry Williamson, contribution to a BBC Radio 4 tribute to James Farrar, *The Unreturning Spring*, (by David Heycock), first broadcast July 1967.

Like Williamson himself, Jim could combine factual fidelity with intense imaginative vision. He smiles in his words: infinitely sweet and kind by nature, his omnivorous delight left unimpaired an inner faculty for remaining uncommitted. This certainly helps him in the RAF reportage which is the main business of his journals and diaries, even some of his letters to his mother. Here we find him collecting, selecting and arranging his material in such a way as to make it of maximum interest. This power of controlled, disciplined observation is as much a Williamson legacy as the vein of nature-mysticism which pervades Jim's more self-conscious 'poetic' prose-style, particularly in its earliest manifestations.

Jim, like HW, had a sensuous and passionate nature. In their dreamy waywardness, feeling for place and love of natural beauty their sensibility was profoundly Celtic: Celtic also in HW's case in the all-pervasive sense of loss, regret for what might have been. Yet lack of inner control would set all at naught, and as we read through Jim's book in chronological sequence (and I have strictly preserved, even occasionally improved – ie, corrected – this aspect of HW's arrangement in making this selection), we can sense him assuming this control with ever-increasing sureness.

In a sense, of course, Jim's phenomenally swift maturity wasn't a natural flowering but a forced growth, like that of other young war-poets, Owen and Keyes for example. The war turned him in double-quick time from an amateur writer into a professional; it also struck him down long before he reached the height of his powers. That is his burden and his mystery. Williamson wrote: '… he is the authentic voice of those who fell in the war, and of those who survived.'

What, now, of this mystic communion between James Farrar and Henry Williamson? This is one of the most fascinating aspects of the Farrar phenomenon. Jim believed that lines of force exist between people, as between poles of a magnet. He read widely when he could and when in the mood – *The Unreturning Spring* contains references to, and sometimes critiques of, writers like Huxley, DH Lawrence, Wilde, Masefield, Philip Gibbs. But if his principal literary forbears were, transparently, men like Edward Thomas and Richard Jefferies, it is almost certain that he discovered these writers – and the composer whose music meant most to him, Frederick Delius – through the agency of his greatest and most influential literary love of all, Henry Williamson. It was first and foremost Williamson's work which stimulated Jim's urge creatively to write himself. 'Once more, having read *The Flax of Dream* with unflagging enthusiasm,' (we find in the early 1940-ish portion of the journal) 'I feel the old restlessness upon me. Like life, this work has its weaknesses, which I see now and did not see before. But by heavens, its beauty, its perception, its moments of untainted inspiration ...! ... it goes deep into my consciousness, like the dream-music of Frederick Delius. If I in my time can create its equal I can go into the earth serenely. "I have planted a tree, made a child, and written a book!"'[1]

Many of Jim's earlier nature-studies are, predictably, little better than imitation Williamson; but as time goes on he becomes more discriminating and learns how to absorb influence as essence, as vital nutrient. In the winter of 1941 he buys four new HWs in the Charing Cross Road – *The Old Stag*; *Goodbye, West Country*; *The Labouring Life* and *The Village Book* – and comments:

> This does not mean that I intend to steep myself in H.W. with the abandon of two years ago, but they are excellent additions to my collection, which now numbers thirteen. It is a collection of great value to me, for I consider it contains some of the finest and most lucid prose of modern times. *Goodbye West Country* is very interesting, as it contains a further development of the reaction against earlier life which was noticeable in *Devon Holiday* and *Linhay on the Downs*. It is an absorbing process; his instance, the irony of his present attitude towards 'fans'. In 1923 and thereabouts the *Flax of Dream* was to be a crusader book to convert humanity: now any fool who happens to have been caught in that ardently-flung net is bashed on the head and thrown back into the sea, unwanted. I'm not saying that his present attitude is unreasonable, having regard for the fact that he still has to work for his bread and butter, and cannot afford to make a sideshow of himself: also that many of these fans, no doubt, are affected young devils who do not appreciate the fundamental earthiness of this writing, which is part of its true value. I don't mean 'earthiness' in its accepted sense, but with an appreciation of the intrinsic value of pristine things.
>
> One can gather from his books that he has very fixed ideas about himself. I would like to learn more details, for instance concerning the technique of sitting in a pub scribbling down songs on matchboxes without being thrown out as a townsman spy. I had often wondered whether Ham was a real village or not, and although I looked it up on several maps I never found it, so I had concluded it wasn't. It is not surprising in the least to have confirmation that his characters are based on actual individuals.[2]

---

[1] *US*, p.45.
[2] *US*, p.48.

Shortly afterwards Jim 'writes up' his poetic prose-piece *Dennis Head*, complete with soaring gulls, bracken, far headlands and Devil's Cauldron.

> ... influenced by the same demigod, but I am not worrying. I wrote it after reading two of his books straight off, and since my interest lies in his handling of words – undoubtedly masterly – as much as in other things, I couldn't really be blamed for having been influenced. I sat up till 2.15 a.m. (I was fire-watching) composing it on the typewriter. In spite of the fact that it's not quite all mine, it's sounder stuff than I've written so far. I enlarged it from a synopsis I had had in my notebook for months, so I *can* claim that I was not moved to do it because of what I had just read. My ambition is to get all the goodness out of H.W. and then lay off to at least a reasonable extent, in order to develop my own methods.[1]

Jim's most eloquent tribute to his 'demi-god', *The Imagination to the Wraith*, is printed on p. 41. No wonder this touched Henry to the quick. Here was young Farrar, sitting on the shingle at Torquay, thinking of Williamson's character Willie Maddison, who is drowned at the end of *The Pathway*: thinking of Willie drowned in the sea, and lamenting it. The irony was that, not long afterwards, Farrar was drowned in the sea himself; and Williamson, the prototype of his hero Maddison whom Jim had been mourning: Williamson was walking about mourning Farrar. This all struck home to Williamson in the aftermath of the war, when he was at his lowest ebb, both mentally and physically. 'Therefore James Farrar meant much to me, and I felt at times that he was helping me. He gave me hope.'[2]

So we come to the heart of the matter. The Farrar/Williamson relationship had some of the elements of master/disciple, but in certain ways was unique. Neither knew the other, save through the medium of the each other's work; the master outlived the disciple; yet Jim, who owed so much in his own art to Henry, in a sense exerted – after his death – a reciprocally creative and sustaining influence on the older writer. Hence the PS scribbled at the top of a postcard to Mrs Farrar, 21 September 1948: 'I have got a nebulous character like Jim (abstraction of my own thought) as U.S.A. pilot in *Phasian Bird*, an early copy, October, which will come to you.' This is the story of a game bird, a rare hybrid pheasant, set in rural Norfolk at the time of the Second

---

[1] *US*, p. 49.
[2] See p. 12, note 6.

World War. In Chapter 24 we read of the blue upper air of the North Sea 'humming with coarse diapason' and of the silver air-fleets leaving multitudinous vapour trails drifting and spreading. One evening, Harra the Denchman (a hoody crow) sees four survivors of a shot-down Fortress aircraft slumped in a dinghy on the sea. One of them came from New England; all his life he had felt a passion for flight, 'which was almost a lyric ecstasy within him ... He was a young man punctilious and high-minded, with ambition to be the poet speaking for his generation as in a previous war Wilfred Owen had spoken for the generation of 1914–18.'[1] The relationship which develops between the 'tall uniformed young man with blue eyes and fair hair'[2] – the airman-poet – and Wilbo, the older, exiled farmer-artist, clearly reflects the bond Williamson felt to exist between him and Jim, whom he never knew in life and had never even heard of while he was living. 'Thus began a friendship between two men which was to continue until death, and even beyond the chiaroscuro of terrestrial living. They shared an inner faith; each gave of himself to the other. The pilot already had penetrated, with the "enlarged and numerous senses" of the poet, to a wider comprehension of reality which was as yet unknown to his fellows.' He thought of the older man 'as one whose light had not been put out by materialism ... they spoke seldom, they understood one another's thoughts, they shared the comradeship of peace.'

Soon the airman must return to his operational unit and affixes to his new ship an enlargement of the painting the older man had given him, of the Phasian Bird in flight. In the wintry December of that year his bomber is badly shot-up in a raid, but limps back home only to

---

[1] HW notes a hint of the young Wilfred Owen in the first lines of Jim's poem *The Wind* (see p. 46); a hint of:

> Leaves
> Murmuring by myriads in the shimmering trees
> Lives
> Wakening with wonder in the Pyrenees.

Reading *The Wind*, with its references to 'blossom unopened', 'fancy unfired', we may well echo HW's surmise: is this JF looking down at himself, knowing that he has no future as an old poet? I'm sure it is: the poets are those who intuitively, that is truly, see, know and understand.

[2] Of V M Yeates, author of *Winged Victory*, Williamson wrote in tribute: 'He had the usual poet's sickness, which killed Keats, Flecker, D.H. Lawrence, Richard Jefferies: bright blue eyes, fair hair, pale, thought-sculptured face ...'
(Introduction to the Sphere Books edition of *Winged Victory*, London 1969, p. 5).

catch fire and crash not far from his friend's farm. The pilot is killed, 'but even as the brains within his skull were bubbling, his spirit was away and beyond the coiling breath, the eddies and the spirals, the white confusion of the Siberian air ... and beholding a golden bird flying to him, bringing upon its breast the sun of far Cathay, the azalea groves and deep rocky ravines noisy with rushing waters, broadening into the wide and reedy valley of the Phasis, a river in Colchis.'

This wasn't to be Jim's only appearance in Williamson's fiction. In *The Gale of World*, the last novel in the *Chronicle of Ancient Sunlight* sequence, the hero Phillip Maddison − Willie's London cousin − is editing in London, in the depressed aftermath of World War II, a literary periodical entitled *The New Horizon* (a fictional counterpart of *The Adelphi*). Some of James Farrar's work is submitted; Philip joyfully accepts and prints it, and, indeed, *After Night Offensive* and a number of other poems and prose-pieces are to be read in the pages of *The Gale of the World* (this interpenetration of fiction and fact is characteristic Williamson).

Williamson saw more in Jim than a writer born to perpetuate his literary ideals and his perception of the world. He would have seen him as an embodiment of his own younger self, thence of his quasi-autobiographical alter ego Willie Maddison − drowned in *The Pathway*, cut off by the tide, after burning his literary masterpiece *The Star Born* in a vain attempt to attract attention. Williamson had to 'murder' Willie in this way before the world could reach him and tarnish his youthful idealism and integrity of outlook − as it had tarnished Williamson's, a sophisticate who yearned to be an innocent again, who would like to have been spared the harsh entry into the adult world where pretension is rife, hopes and promises fail, life ails and ages and relationships founder.[1] This James Farrar was also spared. Like Willie Maddison, Jim perished in the sea; and Williamson knew that the sea cleanses absolutely.[2]

Not that Jim would ever have become a misfit like Willie; for, as we have already noted, and as Henry must have recognised (it would have all been part of the Farrar fascination), Jim's war brought about his maturity; it did not merely arrest his development, as it arrested

---

[1] See Daniel Farson, *Henry: an Appreciation of Henry Williamson*, London 1982, pp. 71–76.
[2] Significantly, it was a copy of 'Willie Maddison's' *The Star Born* that Williamson chose to present 'to the mother of James Farrar, poet, who died in battle, July 1944.'

Henry's and Willie's, leaving them in a state of suspended animation between boyhood and manhood. Jim was probably more essentially adult than either of them. War was a crucial factor. Williamson's discovery of Richard Jefferies' *Story of my Heart* may have been a crystallisation point in his life; but his experiences at the Front had already left permanent scars, and he was forever haunted by the famous Christmas fraternisation between German and English troops in the trenches in 1914, at which he had been present. It needed all the 15 volumes of *A Chronicle of Ancient Sunlight* definitively to work the Great War out of his system. His editing of the stricken pilot V M Yeates' novel *Winged Victory* was all part of the process, and so was the part that he played in bringing the work of James Farrar to the world — and remember that Jim died without the slightest public recognition for his genius.[1] Small wonder that Williamson wrote: 'The new truths are the old truths. We are indeed members one of another.'[2] Another 'member' was Lance-Corporal Walter Robson, killed in North Africa in 1945. In 1960 Williamson found a publisher for, and wrote an introduction to, his war letters, for which he had a very high regard (*Letters from a Soldier*).

Finally we have to consider Williamson's role as intermediary between Jim and his favourite composer, Frederick Delius. Delius (1862–1934) was born in Bradford of Prussian parents but spent most of his life abroad, chiefly in France. His main inspiration was nature, whether the moors of his native Yorkshire, the swamps and river-landscapes of Florida, the mountains of Norway, or the Impressionist country about the Ile de France, where he made his home. His works are nearly all nature-poems — small, medium and large — with evocative titles like *North Country Sketches, The Song of the High Hills, On Hearing the First Cuckoo in Spring, A Song of Summer, In a Summer Garden, Summer Night on the River, Songs of Sunset*. In his artistic and personal outlook, no less than in his poetic feeling for nature, Delius was very much at one with Williamson, Jefferies, James Farrar. Their passionate

---

[1] Of course Jim had no opportunity to revise or correct his work for publication. I have resisted the temptation to tamper editorially, except in a few minor matters of punctuation.

[2] HW's final act of homage to Jim (in 1967) was to arrange for Mrs Farrar to deposit Jim's manuscripts in Exeter University Library, which also received a large number of Williamson's own manuscripts, typescripts and effects. At this time he wrote to Mrs Farrar that Jim's collection 'would be valued ... the more for its quality and fidelity to an older writer, who is himself not without fidelity to the younger writer.'

response to the natural world was in no way diminished by disbelief in the 'God' of popular religious contrivance. Yet they are all deeply 'religious' in the sense that they aspire and look through nature to some immanent spiritual reality, unseen and unknown.

Delius's natural *harmony*, in the widest sense − the belief, attested in his music, that sunlight, country and open air are the natural home of men, his calm, balance, order − these make a more powerful appeal than ever today: to musicians like Ronald Stevenson, for instance, who has recently written (of the *Mass of Life*): 'I have never heard such ecstasy from a choir ... I hear in (Delius's) music a great shout of joy in life ... and a serenity so rare in our century, a security born from contemplation of solitude and far distances ... in an age when men rape the earth, Delius's love of nature is even more salutary today than during his lifetime. The wine of his music has matured.'

These are the reactions of a contemporary composer, an artist;[1] sixty, seventy years ago another artist, not merely music-loving but of an intuitively musical sensibility in the fullest, widest meaning of the term, heard Delius speaking his own language. When Williamson visited Florida in the early 1930s, 'we passed groves of orange trees, and thoughts arose of Delius, who in youth came to Florida to grow oranges − Delius who loved the sun, and dreamed of sunshine, and those sun-fruits which came from whitest bridal bloom − Delius whose music is love and dream and serenity and impersonal heart-ache for starry beauty in life.'[2] Henry's first choice of music as Roy Plomley's guest on *Desert Island Discs* was Delius's setting of Ernest Dowson's *Cynara* − a favourite poem of Aunt Millicent Fairfax in *The Dream of Fair Women*.[3]

There can be little doubt that Jim inherited his own love of Delius from Williamson. The title-page of his journal carries some lines from Whitman as a motto:

---

[1] *Tempo*, 151 (December 1984), p. 27.
[2] *The Linhay on the Downs* (London 1934), p. 292.
[3] I have often wondered if Williamson was aware that Dowson is buried in Ladywell Cemetery. The suburb of Ladywell (in South-East London) was where Henry grew up and is the setting of the early novels in the *Chronicle of Ancient Sunlight* sequence. Henry would have been 5 when Dowson died in 1900; the former's home in what he calls 'Hillside Road' in the *Chronicle* is minutes away from the cemetery.

And every day I, a curious boy, never too close, never
    disturbing them,
Cautiously peering, absorbing, translating.

These are from *Out of the Cradle Endlessly Rocking*, and are set by
Delius in one of his greatest works, *Sea Drift*. Other lines from the
same poem get drawn in to the injured airman's delirium in the short
story *Johnny Beyond* (see p. 71). Delian overtones begin to feature in
Jim's work quite early on. The larks' 'song of summer' towards the
end of 'April 1940' (see p. 24) is an obvious cue for Delius. In *Oldest
Inhabitant* the eponymous hero's[1] local pub is the 'Paradise Garden';
an inn of the same name is featured in the last scene of Delius's opera
A Village Romeo and Juliet and provides the title of one of the composer's loveliest shorter pieces, the interludial *Walk to the Paradise
Garden*. Then we find some brief random entries in Jim's notebook:
one entitled 'Cuckoo in Spring', the next – and this is the first time
he mentions his hero specifically by name – 'The Songs of Delius':

subtle, intangible. The last chord before despair, but yet never despair

– which shows that, though barely eighteen, Jim had already divined
the life-affirming quality in Delius's lyricism which many mistake for
self-indulgence.

Towards the end of his life Delius became blind and paralysed and
totally dependent, for the continuing of his work, on his young
Yorkshire-born amanuensis Eric Fenby. In 1935, after Delius's death,
Fenby published his account of their unique relationship, *Delius as I
knew him*. Both Jim and his brother devoured the book the moment
they could acquire it from the library, and the short story *Episode in
August* – once described by critic Nigel Nicolson as 'a sketch of
wonderful and terrifying originality' – is clearly influenced by Fenby's
vivid descriptions of the garden at Grez-sur-Loing (the tiny hamlet
outside Fontainebleau where Delius lived). The figure of the grandfather

---

[1] Drowned, in the end, in the Atlantic. Another literary premonition, like the death-by-drowning
of Willie Maddison? The business of drowning seems to be a recurrent leitmotif in the assorted
life-work of Delius, Williamson, Farrar. Williamson's favourite music of all was Wagner's
Tristan and Isolde, in which the lovers in their death-*extasis* are implicitly claimed by the sea;
firstborn of this was Delius's *Village Romeo and Juliet*, in which the two child-lovers drown
together in a hay-filled barge rather than accept the world and adulthood, with all its compromise
and disillusion. Very Williamsonian-Maddisonian.

is modelled on Delius himself, who on still, warm days would sit motionless in his chair in the garden, revelling in the atmosphere and silently worshipping the sun. Not all the physical details tally – for example, Delius had no beard – but this is a novelist's privilege. The point is that the vital forces of memorable characters in fiction are nearly always drawn from actual life.

Delius was not the only composer Jim admired. He responded warmly also to Ravel (*Jeux d'Eau* and *Daphnis et Chloë*), to Elgar (the *Enigma Variations*), even to Stravinsky (more guardedly).[1] But Delius remained his number-one favourite. He constantly makes memorable discoveries:

> After much labour have managed to get a secondhand copy of Flecker's *Hassan* ... It is grand: dramatic and beautiful, not forgetting the necessary asset of humour. What a production it must have been with Delius's music – and to think it was presented full-length on the wireless when I had never heard of it, and just listened casually.[2]

Frederick Delius died in June 1934, just over ten years before his young admirer. Yet in a sense he had already written Jim's epitaph. In 1915, in the midst of that earlier holocaust in which Williamson was a combatant, Delius had completed his *Requiem*, dedicated 'to the memory of all young artists fallen in the war'.[3] Jim can't have known it since it was performed only once before he died (in 1922) and 'killed by the Christians' (Ernest Newman to Felix Aprahamian). Yet it's exactly the kind of In Memoriam that Jim would have wanted – not a hymn of mourning for the dead, but a paean to life and living, to the green goodness of the earth, to Williamson's 'lovely spirit abiding in men's hearts'. The first two movements bid us be mindful of the days of darkness, which shall be many, and not to clog our minds and hearts with mendacious life-denying nonsense; the third is an early-summer-morning love-song; in the fourth the parting spirit is

---

[1] Conversely, at least one composer has been moved to set some of Jim's poems to music. Trevor Hold's *The Unreturning Spring*, a song-cycle for soprano, baritone and chamber orchestra, was published by the University of Wales Press in 1965.

[2] *US*, pp. 123–4.

[3] As a result of participating in that unofficial Christmas Eve 'truce' in 1914, Williamson was forever unable to regard the Germans as the Enemy. Delius, being of German origin, was painfully involved in conflicting loyalties when Europe went to war and friends and family and their offspring faced each other as unwilling foes.

re-absorbed, Jefferies-like, into nature; and the finale blesses the eternally renewing power of spring, of spring returning:

> Eternal renewing! Everything on earth will return again. Springtime, summer, autumn and winter – and then comes new springtime!

But why am I writing about music, which you cannot hear off the printed page? Why not merely turn to the eighteen-year-old poet James Farrar, to his 'Two Songs of Autumn':

(1)

Brave roadside ragwort scurried under wind.
　　The mad meadow grass where mildewed agony
Spews forth crows like ghouls
　　Clanking the hedge-eddies with fingered spread.
The hedge-dank leaf-fouled lane before me falls
　　To a dead distance of hills and sky.

Struggle under the writhing wood which a mile back
　　Roared like a sea. The lustful air,
Harvesting shoals of jaundice from frenzied oak,
　　Plucks vainly at the slow arc-tracing pines.
Stand in a devil-darkness of leaves and smoke,
　　Shin-deep. Wild branches scream despair
At the full thunder of the drowning year.

(2)

A caravan comes up the lane: old horse cringing
　　Like a tired insect in its slow grief.
Bleached painted sides, lean leathern gipsy driving:
　　Old woman and blind son with bitter mouths curled.
Yet the lean one turns with lit face; his voice peals
　　'Bound away north. Back in spring, in spring!'
Thralled, I watch them away under the hills
　　In the tunnel of darkness, the dying world.

Break fibre, raise and fly leaf!
　　Rise, in the wind's lusting mouth sing –
Soar and shout, to the faint stars away!
　　I care not that night comes cold or the dead sun
Droops on the earth in the short weak day –
　　Back in Spring, in Spring!

CHRISTOPHER PALMER
London, St John's Wood
Midsummer 1985

Extracts from
'The Unreturning Spring'

April 1940

The night sky is clear, without the frost-glitter of winter. Spica is flaming up through the eastern sky, and Orion is conquered. He no longer strides, but trails down into the horizon, dragging an unwilling Sirius. These spirit-quenched stars seem to have yielded up their strength into the sun by day.

The first blossoming, as usual, comes very suddenly: one day, it seems, there is a strangeness in the almond trees, and the next they rise in spires of pink to the fresh-coloured sky. They stand out dazzlingly along the road, trees hitherto never noticed.

Along the lanes the sun falls hot, casting beautiful hedgerow-shadows: starlings call 'wheeeooo' from the rooftops of the scattered houses, and sparrows squat contentedly in the gutters. Distant trees, starkly blue-brown in winter, are now dusted with light green. The woods themselves show definite changes. The undergrowth is thicker in green – which gives a wrong impression: there, too, it is sparse as yet – than the trunks above, where the grey-green of birch seems too delicate to exist, and gleaming chestnut buds curve up at the end of their twigs like great upright chandeliers. Starlings flash about on sun-transparent wings, and pigeons beat swiftly and straitly overhead: while over the sown fields, the vegetables and the fallow land, the lapwing rears and tumbles, white-gleaming, on great rounded wings, calling wildly in its fluting whistle.

From now on there is alternate rain and strong sunshine, and the grass grows lush in the mowing-meadows. I went for a round tour, and with a great thrill heard the first cuckoo in the Oaks Park,[1] on the 21st; by now the trees were beginning to get massy in foliage, and celandines were everywhere. The voice of the cuckoo, having made itself noticed, refused to leave me, but at the bottom of the holdings my

---

[1] The countryside round Jim's home in Carshalton in Surrey is the setting of these pieces, and of 'September 1940' and 'The Hayfield' which follow.

attention was removed by a beautiful sight. Bleached telegraph posts spired up from the new growths of nettles: on the singing wire, above and behind the untidy elderberries, sat a swallow. It flipped its wings and preened them, in utter nonchalance of its wanderings from Africa; head and shoulders gleaming richly and darkly against the sky, it sang and spread its tail. Then it was gone in a fierce swoop, tumbling and dashing with its mate in the sun: between the trees, in and among the sties and outhouses: tails flexing and the song of summer pouring from their throats.

Now the pure sky is milk-stained with high cirrus, and the spring wind stirs the ruins of last summer's flowers: sunlight is richly hot and I can lie in fresh grass and feel the great curvature of the earth thrusting me to the unseen stars. Lying in the sun, I always find this, that the earth seems to fall away all round me.

Dandelions are in sudden profusion, and ground ivy blossoms with small purple bell-flowers. The yellow flags in the pond seem to grow inches every day, and daffodils showily flourish and pass: I do not really care, for they mean less to me than the celandine and the ground ivy.

* * * * *

May

... The chestnut blossom, which has been standing in pink spires upon the trees, is now a brown carpet to the road. The first umbellifers, beaked parsley, are everywhere along the hedges, in tremendous profusion: bitter-sweet and bryony also begin to twine in the stubby branches above them. I now make a habit of going out very late, nearly every Friday evening. The first occasion, at the end of May, is devoid of real pleasure. It is too overcast, and the woods, so well-known by daylight, are an impenetrable mass under this sullen sky. Towards midnight there is a clearing in the southern sky, and with great pleasure I see Scorpio thrusting up: even so, it is hardly the night for such an event, and the red first-magnitude star is almost white. So I cast my thoughts back to that greater occasion last year, when I only saw Antares for the first time late in the summer, when the woods were rich and the fields mottled with drifts of campions.

Three different bells toll midnight, and in the silence afterwards the dark earth and sky droop in a dead calm: beneath the unwinking constellations and the great scarf of the Milky Way I wait with hardly a breath, feeling, rather than hearing, something like the whisper of the blood in my ear-drums. It is the guns in France.

The sky nowadays is commanded by the swifts. In the hot mornings they wheel and wheel incessantly, high up in a vault which gradually becomes more and more bronzed and then white-hot, and quite suddenly is an overcast mass of great blinding thunder-clouds. On the darkness of the threatening storm they are silhouetted even darker, still circling, until, again quite suddenly, the steeled strength of the sky gives, and it splits away into a mosaic of pearly rags, which dwindle in the deepening blue. When these last, calmer clouds begin to flush with the sunset, the swifts come down in all their multitudes, screaming reedily, and streak in frantic groups round the trees and among the houses.

* * * * *

June

Lying in Hill Field one very hot day, I see two stoats venturing out on to the path after much crashing about in the undergrowth. Although within eight or nine feet of me they are unaware of my presence and swagger off into the grass, where I can hear them coursing about for some time.

My next night tour is almost unsurpassable. It is calm and moonlit, and the hedgerows gleam with those night-flowers, the campions. Thinking of their peculiar perfume, I decided that somehow it had not only a message for the nose, but also a *colour*. Thus it always strikes me that campions have a soft pink scent, honeysuckle a thick yellow-crimson scent, elderberry a grey scent, heliotrope a 'chocolate-purple' scent, and mock-orange an icy, white-yellow scent.

The world is rich in unexpected scents now.

Going along the hedges I have several times seen hedgehogs aimlessly muddling about in the open. They must be about the most difficult animals to kill or hurt in cold blood.

Along the borders of the wood I walk in stubble, for the land is rich with the scent of the mown hay, which now lies in swathes. Large roses gleam high up in the vegetation together with strangely scented platters of elderberry blossom, and below them are great rank cow-parsnips, eight, ten and twelve inches across.

Many times I pause and examine the creamy waxen rose petals in the moonlight, and sample the elusive scent, debating the alleged superiority of the great slimy, copper-coloured garden roses, with stench like a scent factory on a hot afternoon in August.

*   *   *   *   *

July
... Silence is the keynote now. The birds have stopped singing, only the lightest of breezes sifts the coined light on the woodland tracks. Alone the turtle dove drowsily worships high summer.

Apart from mallows and the ever-flowing campions, there is not much to distinguish the hedgebanks now. From now on the prevailing colour is yellow. The bright novelty of May's cups and tubes and stars and platters is now no more than a tangled dryness: a gaunt-armed skeleton with tufted fingers: a mat of leafage bored and runnelled by grubs. Ragged are the flowers now, by chalk-dump and roadside: a dusty poppy here and there catches the eye, petals flapping like red butterflies' wings at the swift passage of a car.

Venturing farther out from the world of brick boxes, however, I find that there is still variety in the less frequented places. Blue chicory flaunts itself in the sun with ragwort and various thistles: on the dry hillsides thousands of sheep's-bit scabious nod in the wind, their small lilac rosettes contrasting with yellow hawkweed. Above all, of course, at this time of year, I notice the thyme matting the ground. On the Wild Hill I have seen this plant growing nearly as big as valerian.

*   *   *   *   *

August
One evening, as small tarry puffs of cloud drifted into the general western conflagration, I went round to Chipstead Valley. Darkness was slow in coming, so I lay on my back on the cropped turf, while the stars gleamed through cirrus cloud. From the steely ashes of the west there arose a strong breeze which rushed along the hillside. The stars burned whiter, shrubs were like sentinels facing the wind: at last the moon rose, and as if at its sign the air became still. Going down the road with unnaturally loud footsteps, I found mystery in the pale flame of moonlight among birch-trunks: a roof across the valley shone like a wet slab. On Wild Hill I sat down again and listened to the hum of

26

the power station I had passed a few moments before. It was very impressive down there, with its roof slanting high against the stars, chinks of light showing at the windows, and its eternal engines turning over as if driving the universe.

Antares, wherefore art thou white — or nearly white? I think I shall have to investigate this phenomenon, which is probably the result of blackout conditions. The whole summer long I have looked at this star, and not once did it have more than a tinge of colour. Strangely enough, our other famous coloured star, Sirius, looked quite normal last winter, although I must admit Aldebaran was a little washed-out.

The swifts have gone early this year: swallows are still in abundance around the harvest-fields and over the village gardens. Nor are they confined to their normal semi-civilized surroundings — barns, out-houses, etc. — for one sees bands of them skimming the surface of the fields in open country, probably after the pale moths and other winged insects which twirl among the stubble.

Have the swifts left already, or is it that the furious gunfire of late has driven them from the urban areas? During heavy barrages by day one can see the confusion among flocks of birds even on the ground, so who can say what the effect of a bursting shell would be on an aerial hunter of the swift's calibre, miles up in the night sky?

A very beautiful feature of my night walks this summer has been the reeling of crickets in the first orchard up the Holdings. The loudest cricket I have ever heard greeted me one night from the vicinity of the farm buildings along the Flying Field track (towards Hill Field). I should say I heard him a hundred yards away. Stepping through the hedge to investigate (and incidentally startling a black cat, blissfully happy in such a rat-infested place) I skirted the barn-and-stable, with cart-shed adjoining, and came into the full moonlight. There he was on a large muck-heap, shouting and shouting into the lunar glare until the night rang with sound.

Bats are very noticeable just now. As well as the little pipistrelle, which is so common up the holdings tracks, I have seen several noctules or barbastelles. They seem very bold, and often when I meet one on a narrow path he tours round me for ten or fifteen minutes, usually flying up the path to a definite landmark such as a tree, then coming back at a fair height: swooping past me with a leathern 'flicker-flacker' of wings and rising again to a similar turning-point at the other end.

Early in the evening they do not venture far from their daytime retreats, as they can be seen flittering in small circles around the upper foliage of trees, plunging in at intervals.

* * * * *

September
With the incoming of September, wild flowers dwindle in variety, so that we are left with the age-old dandelion, many ragworts, and struggling poppies (many pinkish and undeveloped). The sun is hot, but beats lower, often arising in a golden haze like a vision of Turner. On the ends of beech-twigs the old wonderful tale begins to be retold.

Old man's beard still flowers, but on many bines the green hairy 'beards' straggle out from the clusters of brown seeds, all pointing inwards like eggs in a tit's nest. Hedgebanks are clotted with thistle-down; strung with the spider's creation (like a mockery of the cow-parsnip flower whose tufted arms are now its foundation).

Heavy dews drip from the trees in the early morning. The moon, tiny in the zenith, weaving a blurred web in the misty darkness, reveals wet patches which break away in runnels over the camber of the road, under every copse.

Flowers in the garden are bright and untidy. Among the drying stems those first drifts of leaves begin to cover the earth.

SEPTEMBER, 1940

I walked endlessly, no clock drips by the hours,
  The burnished hedgerows, clotted and high,
The still woods, the dead meadows, the closed flowers,
  Shrunken under that bright scarred sky.

A light-play, as of sun on August leaves,
  A height-soft moan, a wooden intermittent rattle,
And, as the scrolled conflict eastward weaves,
  Feelers drooping darkly out of battle.

They come slowly, soft tap-roots questing down,
  At the groping tip of one glisters a bead of light:
I see them, like waterflies struggling not to drown,
  Soundlessly pass into earth, and meet night.

What is it that they are fallen?
  Sane men hold it to be just
That each, when dead feed the earth like pollen,
  Lies strewn in some broken field in a wrack of dust.

* * * * *

The Hayfield (in retrospect)
On the eastern side of the woods is a sloping plain called Hill Field.
Seen with the telescopic vision of extreme youth it was, I remember,
a prairie, but it dwindled as my stature increased and resolved itself
into a large, ragged field, indisputably finite and limited in possibilities
of adventure.

At the bottom, which is fringed with great elms, two vague trenches
begin to wander towards the centre of the field. There is no apparent
reason for their presence: perhaps they were an attempt to lay a pipe-
line to nowhere in particular. At any rate they were abandoned, and
are now evident by the broken chalk ramparts like great trails of bird-
droppings, half-overgrown with the coarse grass which is Nature's scab
for wounds. Among other flowers, poppies impart a Flanders touch
to these ancient scars.

Through many seasons this land has been untended. I remember it,
glorious with deep drifts of umbellifers and clouds of campions, in past
summertimes; I remember it brown and ruinous with the skewed wrack
of summer's flower-stalks; I remember it leaden with the sky, deep in
snow. And always it has been wild, the grazing-place of gipsy horses.

Last year the grass came up thickly, and was trodden by few. I used
to see it nearly every evening, just a little greener and a little richer,
and all the while heightening. The cuckoo came to the woods, and the
field was virulent to greet it. Swallows hawked over the grasses for tiny
moths which wandered there, and after a few weeks young skylarks
rose into the air among them. Now the grass was a yard high and
foaming with flower. The long evening shadows of the trees floated
purple, as if on an ocean of whitish-green, and walking through it I
was showered with pollen-dust.

Sometimes I would lie on my back in the depths of the grass, revelling
in the light of the evening sky, which came down to me through a
sweetness of translucent stems. Then I would tire of the sky, and turn
sideways into a green submarine world. Darnel, timothy grass, rye grass,
wall barley, quaking grass, cocksfoot — all these were around me, with
white campions borne among the thick low growth. The stalks were
frothed with cuckoo-spit; spiders and tiny flies battled in a jungle of
leaves and white moths spun aimlessly above them.

The tree shadows sank again across the field, and soon the pollen
was gone. Now the grass-stalks took more strength from the sun,

becoming ribbed and hard, while the seed-heads lost their greenness and turned to light mauve, brown, gold: the gold was ominous, and one day while I was working in the hellish whirr of London another kind of whirr was sounding in Hill Field.

I next came there at night. The moon was full in a clear sky and, standing very still, I could hear a sound like the whisper of blood in my ear-drums: the guns in France. The hayfield was a calm sea of stubble, the swathes like white breakers ribbed across it. I lay in one of those swathes for nearly an hour, under the faint steady stars and the scarf of the Milky Way, drowsing in the sweetness of the hay which, strangely, gave me the sun by night. There is a stored sunlight in hay which time and darkness do not destroy. In the dried grass beneath me and around me were little withered thistle spikes, snakes of convolvulus, broken fluted spars of parsley, the dark blur of dead poppies.

The hay was carried and became lop-sided ricks in the yard beyond the hedgerow elms. Soon afterwards army huts went up in the woods and heavy lorries careered round the edge of the field, making a mire of the stubble when the rain came. During the autumn and winter, when tens of thousands of missiles were scattered on London, and the docks became virtually empty, the cry for home production arose. The Government adopted a policy of 'Back to Golden Corn – Even in a Grass Country,' and Hill Field went under wheat. The bright round-tipped leaves came through late, but there was rain all spring through and now the weather has broken fine the wheat is rising with slow strength. I have seen its progress from the time when it was almost lost in the great clumsy clods and half-buried yellow grass of land which has probably not been broken since the last war. Now the field is a flame-bright yellow from hedge to hedge with the charlock released by the plough: I suppose eventually the wheat will come into its own among these gipsy plants which battle still with the rising stems. Patriotism cannot, thank God, be instilled into flowers.

I am sorry when I remember the hay of last year, but though the face of the land is vicious with conflict like that of the pre-war wilderness and the wartime wheat, fundamentally there is little change. The blossom goes into dust from the hedgerows, ranks of cow-parsnips stand white along the roadsides, swifts sing of their hot sky, and the sweetness of summer is upon the earth.

*   *   *   *   *   (*Spring 1941*)

OLDEST INHABITANT

I

A little swarthy labourer in a dark green tweed suit entered the pub known as the 'Paradise Garden', and stood shuffling his feet on the mat, blinking and peering round at the gathering while his eyes accustomed themselves to the light. His face was set in a perpetual half-grin, his mouth sardonic: while his bright eyes, under heavy black brows, glanced good-humouredly around at the scene. He took it all in, the rosy innkeeper snapping the tops off bottles, the motley crew propped against the counter, the leaping fire with other men gathered around the wide hearth, old granfers in the corner: burnished brass, a jumble of cheap china ornaments and old darts on the mantelshelf, prints of horses on the timbered walls, the blue fug hiding the ceiling.

'Evenun, chaps', he said at last.

There was a buzz of greeting, and glasses were lowered as he went over to the counter, his steel-studded boots clanking and slurring on the stone floor. Everyone was quiet now. They all watched him as he took his pint and, having flourished it in their direction, lowered it while his green trilby hat with the budgerigar feather in it fell to the floor behind him. With great deliberation he picked up the hat, dusted it off, and placed it on the counter. Turning to the silent groups of men, while the innkeeper stopped wiping glasses and leaned over the wet counter to watch him, he said slowly:

'Wull now, gennulmen, I zeen th'ould man isself. Pitiful though 'tis, pore ould feller, I doan't reckon ter zee'n comin' dru this winter.'[1]

There was a chorus of disappointed 'Oh's' and babel broke loose. He viewed the excited villagers with lofty tolerance for a few moments, and then raised his hand, at which signal the bubbub subsided.

'Yes, chaps, pore ould John Wedgewick. Holdest man in the village. Ninety-three years 'as 'e bin 'pon this mortal earth,' continued the little man dramatically. ''N 'tis some shameful fer ter zee'n laid thurr sayin' as his life be done. Shameful, 'tis.'

'Now, 'Appy Isaac, you'm looking' fer a 'ole fer ter put'n in,'

---

[1] No doubt HW's Devon books helped Jim with his notation of West Country dialect, of which his time in Manaccan gave him some first-hand knowledge.

remarked the innkeeper pointedly. 'You 'n th'ould vulture in the corner.'
There was much laughter.

'Ay, set'n in praper, Isaac,' came the soft voice of a rheumy old
man in the corner, muffled up to the neck in an old Army great-coat.
His pale eyes were watering.

'That's right, Isaac,' said a big shock-headed man who drove the
corn-lorry. ''Twill be a budiful vuneral, all they dark suits. Dear ole
Vicar with ees 'air wavin' over the grave as th'ould man goes down.'

'Now looky yurr, Isaac Curnow,' came another voice, 'you'n they
two graveyard 'awks didn't ought ter consider yerselves fit fer the
comp'ny of this 'ostlry.' (Approving cries.) 'Tidden sif the man were
gone yet-awhiles. Gord am' ut, man, you're on'n afore 'e's took ees
boots off!''

'Doan' worry 'bout they 'eathens, Isaac,' came an urgent voice from
the old man. 'Us've gotter find'n a place.'

'Surenuff,' said Isaac, who was the gravedigger. 'Us've gotten a
praper praper li'l place fer'n, budiful, 'tis. Up by th'edge, wi' th'helms
lookin' down on'n. Oh, and the flowers'll grow some lovely, an' the
grass come up like 'twas a meader.'

'Budiful,' murmured the old man in the corner, rapturously rocking
himself to and fro.

Actually they all liked nothing better than a wedding or a funeral.
Every farmer and labourer could don his one and only best suit, and
groups of almost silent men would walk discreetly to church, while the
wives, unrecognizable behind archaic veils and hiding their practical
hands in gloves, talked clothes to eternity. Then the ceremony: the Vicar,
a boisterous man out of church, proudly declaring some agitated young
couple man and wife while the female congregation wept. Or, if the
occasion was a burial, standing over the grave with his long black hair
wind-tangled, booming mournfully: Isaac Curnow in the famous green
suit beside him.

The graveyard attracts all the social life of the village.

2

After the nurse left the room, the old man lay quietly in his ancient
bed, watching the candle-flame twist and jump, and listening to the
river sounds outside. Although he was so old his sight and hearing were
remarkably good.

He heard her moving about downstairs, collecting her coat and basket and finally closing the door behind her. The candle-flame shuddered, then continued to burn upright: he was alone with his thoughts and they, by their immensity and variety, told him he was dying.

Slowly he turned his head and looked round the room. He had refused to have the place touched after it had happened. There was the wash-stand with water that had stood a week in the basin and had a film of dust on it: two moths floated spread-winged. The surface looked sluggish in the candle-light, like thick oil. The jug lay in pieces on the floor where he had dropped it; a few withered asters scattered around. He had brought them in from his garden just previously, and, having no bowl, arranged them in the water-jug. He washed seldom enough, anyway.

His gaze ran over the threadbare carpet, where a mouse was ponder-ing, and rested upon his one chair, an ornate, stained thing with the rush seat broken through where he had staggered and rested that day. It stood by the window opposite him, seeming to shudder on its bowed legs as the candle-flame jerked. Apart from these and the high brass bedstead in which he now lay, he had no other furniture in the room. The walls were covered with a faded pink paper representing trelliswork with roses endlessly spattered upon it: if he looked at it too long it seemed to pulsate at him, though he had known it for fifty-six years. Decoration consisted of one picture of a sailing-ship, for John Wedgewick was a Plymouth man and had seen most of the world from the decks of a windjammer.

Sighing, he laid his head jerkily back on the pillow. He was bald, but an ample white beard covered most of his stringy neck. The frail bronze of his face was still fairly smooth, although the features had sunken and jutted according to the shape of the skull: his washed-out eyes seemed to have taken on a new brightness, which was false. But the ancient body, still clad in shirt and trousers, felt hardly a part of him.

As he lay there, and various features of the room made shadowy gestures at him as the candle flickered, he began to dream. The pink wallpaper, the tiny window which could hardly have been opened with a mallet, the view beyond of the dark hillside across the river − all these went into darkness, and his mind was filled with a great sunlight.

It was like the revelation of childhood which all men seek in after life, but never find.

He was happy, living again like this, and to aid the reality he reached out a shaking arm and quenched the candle-flame. With the smoky smell of the hot wax, the tiny red eye of wick looking at him from the darkness, other thoughts impressed themselves upon him. The vast slack sails of the barque *Herzogin Cecilie*, during a race of the grain-ships from Australia, was a sight he had somehow never forgotten: it was driven into his mind by the fact that they had hung, three ships together, not five hundred yards apart for four days, during which the respective crews had resorted to every form of sorcery and cheerful blasphemy to try and break the uncanny gregariousness existing between their ships. At last the calm spell broke and the Finnish barque moved away amid loon-like cries of frantic sailors. Now as he lay dying a great lump arose in his throat for the sea.

More visions. Quays in winter sunlight, sails and loose rigging fretting across his brain, writhing phosphorescent seas, listless voices of drowned seamen: the rainbow of a flying-fish leaping – the shock of scintillating drops brought him to himself, and he lay again hearing the quiet gabble of the tide outside the cottage: moist-faced, staring into darkness.

Bright flowers begin to move at him, nebulous faces, fuming wreaths of smoke ...

3

At about three o'clock an owl flew past the window skirling, and wakened him. He lay stupidly, hearing the faint cries of other owls far off in the night. After some minutes he became aware of another sound, like the 'sock, sock' of wavelets against the bows of a boat. With this there was a fast-running jumble of light musical sounds, with an occasional thump or crackle, while farther off a constant surge filled the night. He lay and pondered, and gradually a brightness came again into his tired eyes, his body thrilling with awareness: raising his head to hear better, he realized that he was feeling clear and light as a kitten. Then he knew that he must go out to watch the tide-race.

He sat up, the excited blood leaving his head, so that he could see nothing: grimly he rested back on his elbows until his vision cleared. Then, feeling madly strong again, he pushed back the blankets and turning on his side pushed his legs over the side of the bed. Deliberately, though without so much ease, he felt for his boots, and pushed his sweating feet into them. Now he was glad he had not let her interfere with the room.

This was the crucial moment. Gently he straightened his bony legs, which had stopped trembling, and pushed himself to his feet. In the darkness, he fumbled for the door-handle, but eventually turned it and opened the door, which whined protestingly. He stood for a moment outside, swaying. The house was dead quiet. But that surge of water outside intoxicated him, so that he could wait no longer. He moved heavily to the top of the stairs and began to lower himself from step to step, grasping at the banisters. He came to the bottom, a fine frenzy taking hold of him, and pulled the door open.

Now it was real, as he staggered into the porchway. The moonlight was madness upon the river, sliding and juggling over the fast-moving ripples, lambent in the shallows. He left the cottage and shuffled across the road to stand above the water, feet rooted in the detritus of flaky shale littered with corks and tins. The water gabbled away past his feet: now and then a cluster of twigs would go past glinting wet, or a streamer of foam. Farther out a great force of water was swirling solidly downriver. Nightbirds shrieked from the darkness of the hillsides, and many curlews fluted above the running tide.

Old John was obsessed by its fine speed and stood reeling on the bank. He began to sing in his weak voice, and a breeze seemed to spring up, softly moving the branches of the trees until a thin whining came from them. As he thought of the seagoing waters in the estuary he broke off his foolish song and sobbed weakly with nostalgia. The water-surge grew louder in his ears, combining with the whine to drown his voice, while leaves seemed to be swirling down at him from all directions. Now the sound was like thunder filling his brain and crushing thought out of existence. He went down in a pulsing redness which ebbed into nullity.

4

For a while it could have been said that only the curlews in the seaward estuary knew the whole truth about that night. Gradually, of course, the people of the village sifted the evidence until the facts became clear for all to see, including the enraged gravedigger: the open cottage door and the deep scores in the riverbank opposite left not much doubt as to what had happened. John Wedgewick had gone out and drowned himself, they say; though they could not conceive what force had driven him, a dying man in his ninety-third year, to leave his bed and commit such a superfluous crime. Anyway, one of the favourite stories in the bar of the 'Paradise Garden' is how the oldest inhabitant of Penloar cheated Isaac Curnow and went back to the Atlantic on the night tide.

(*Autumn 1941*)

From a work un-named and un-written
... I cannot tolerate the blasphemy, which is to create a white image, and place it behind the stars, and call it God. I cannot accept tolerance of turpitude and stupidity, which decimates a generation, saying it is ordained: of a society whose logic is to follow religious inhibition of the body with a denunciation of harlotry: and of an octopus of wealth, rampant over half the world, which can go to worship on a chosen day and grasp its salvation, mouthing 'The humble and the meek.'

There is no God for me, no idolatry of self-excusal. But I am not blind, nor without wit: I try to walk in the light, speaking truth, truth which is poison to some. At times I perceive clearly a spirit behind the sun; and sometimes the world is no more than earth, and all is illusion.

I do not know whether Christ lived; if he lived he was a genius, and as a genius was destroyed by the world of men, to whom such greatness seems distasteful. Now his doctrines are forgotten by the mass of professing followers.

My belief is of old time, being reborn with myself. Herein, and not hereafter, shall I seek salvation.

23 February 1942
We are in a block of flats about half a mile from Lord's Cricket Ground, and close to the Zoo. It is bare and rough-and-ready, but we are doing nicely for ourselves. I am in a room with three other chaps, and we mix in well. We have had nothing much yet except for a lot more filling-in of forms, kit dishes-out, various parades for no apparent reason, and (this afternoon) a dental inspection. It is all a bit of a flurry at present, but we are settling down and I like it tremendously. Eating is a hectic business. We go to the Zoo and have to eat a full meal in about ten minutes because hundreds of chaps are coming in the whole time: they deal with literally thousands each mealtime. We often have

to queue up. They dish out the stuff plate by plate and we go past grabbing it in cafeteria style. We get cheese-potato pie often as a filler-upper, which is something like macaroni cheese in taste; sausages, spinach and other quite succulent things, and to-day I actually had some fruit pudding and custard which was really up my street. Of course they have got vast ovens and special equipment, which makes all the difference. The mugs of tea are about six inches high and four or five across, and must hold as much as five of our teacups. I believe they put bromide or something in the tea to counteract the 'constipatory' effect of Service food.

I suppose the garden at home will begin to improve shortly now. I'd love to see the almond tree blossoming this year; perhaps I will. It all seems very remote now to think of spring and what it means, but no doubt the cut-off feeling will diminish to some extent as I become used to the life. I remember when I started in the accountants' office I went through a peculiar stage in which I was unable to enjoy the evening as my own part of the day. Somehow I was so tied up in the work – involuntarily of course – that I couldn't get free in the intervals between one day's work and another. It's like that here: one can't get absorbed in any but factual matters, but I like to think of how lovely it will be when the door opens a little and the sunlight comes in. I know that it will only deepen my appreciation of what I intend to make my own living interest when all this is over, therefore I am content. I am beginning to understand more of the truth about H.W. now.

I have just got my much-coveted V.R.[1] badges to sew on the sleeves of tunic and greatcoat, so I must put aside my journal and get on with the sewing.

* * * * *

March 1942
On Thursday I and three others were packed off to Euston House in a hurry, and there we had the Radio-Observer Selection Board. They failed two of us and passed two. Then I had to go through the full flying medical all over again, but was lucky and came through O.K. On Friday I had to go up again to complete the medical (they hung me up

---

[1] Volunteer Reserve.

overnight to get the result of my chest X-ray, checking up on my medical history of tuberculosis). Then I rushed back to Abbey Lodge for a vision test. (They will supply me with special corrected goggles for flying!) And after a lot more messing-about I was informed that I would be posted. So on Saturday off we went.

We did a forced march from St. John's Wood to Paddington wearing full kit. We survived, however, and came down non-stop on a troop-train. After about fifty miles out from London, the weather began to clear, and soon I was gazing at some of the most lovely scenes I have ever seen from a train, clear-cut and beautiful in brilliant sunshine, the real rural Wiltshire, meandering water-ways, the soft green turf, ruddy ploughland, trees like etchings against a clear sky.

When we got to Torquay it was like June in everything except heat. This is a lovely place. It is all up hill and down dale, white houses with green shutters along the roads (nearly all hotels). But the main attraction is seawards. From the window of our room we have a magnificent view of, first, our gardens, spacious, beautifully kept by cadets, smooth lawns and red earth beds: beyond this tennis courts and all around terraces of white buildings down the hillsides to the sea.

Discipline is strict. We work from 8 a.m. to 6 p.m. There are many rules and regulations and very little chance to get around: those Devon lanes in spring may not see me after all, I'm afraid! It really is work here, with a vengeance, and even when we've finished instruction for the day we are not through. It is an eight-week course, shortened therefore intensive, and we must pass all exams to get our LAC.[1] In addition to work there are barrack-room jobs, inspections, guards duties, etc.

I am writing this in and around a fine NAAFI supper of scrambled eggs on toast, chips, coffee, bread and marg. and two flat Scotch biscuits − 10½d. At Lord's the NAAFI in our building was a rotten place, run by two girls whom one could only in all fairness call bitches: they treated the RAF like dirt. Here, however, we are most fortunate. The NAAFI is only just about twenty-five yards down our road and sells good stuff with cheerful service. The prices are amazingly low − last night I had sausages and chips, cocoa, bread and marg. and a cake for 8½d. I come in here each night for a supper as we have nothing after high tea at 6 o'clock: lots of other chaps do the same.

---

[1] Leading Aircraft Man.

Excerpt from Standing Orders *re* off-duty hours: 'Airmen must walk in quick time, in step, not more than two abreast. Airmen must not lounge or window-gaze. Airmen must not walk arm-in-arm with females,' etc., etc. I have come across one very decent person on the administrative side — the padre. He is quite a high officer — Wing-Commander — but in the little I have so far seen of him he shows himself to be an honest-to-God Christian. He is the human type, dark with telling thick eyebrows and a thoroughly decent face. He is sometimes seen about the place chatting and joking with the humble cadets in the best of good fellowship.

There is no trouble about what to do with myself here. In the evening I find it pleasant to walk alone. I had a walk round by the sea last night — perfect peace in my own company. The front is all barbed wire, etc., but I could get down on to the sands — the sand is the colour of old fishing-smack sails — and what with the quiet sea and the gulls and the happy Sunday-night promenaders I was very happy myself at sunset. I am beginning to get used to the life, which means that I can act more like a human being when off duty. I was surprised to find I had the desire to write, which I sat down and did in the sunshine.

Oh, how good it is just to sit writing with time on my hands. I feel no homesickness. I had wondered before I left whether I would get terribly smitten and miserable, but it hasn't been like that at all. No misery gnawing at my innards, just a deep appreciation of home which is quite mature and well-disciplined. Therefore I am happy here and home-loving at the same time, which is a very nice feeling.

THE OLD LIFE

The time we cycled from Truro to Manaccan in the evening, which was quite the loveliest ride I have ever had: trudging up the hills with all my well-known June flowers by the roadside, campions red and white, Herb Robert, Cornish stonecrop and foxglove, woodbine and bryony in the hedges: multitudes of others passed unknown as we rushed downhill in the cool of the evening, with all the fields brimming with sunset light and a heavy incense of honeysuckle filling the lanes.

Then the early morning walks round Woodmansterne about the time of greatest dawn-song, in May. The early-lit lanes proud with ranks of white hedge-parsley and gix, all fresh stems and bright soft umbels in the sunlight: merry morning whistle of sparrows, perhaps a swift already on high like a lord of the summer sky over the empty fields.

To enter the woods by the northern end is to be engulfed in a Mediterranean brilliance of sifted light-play. The upper parts of the trees held against the sun in a vibrant yellow haze in which hidden jays scream: lower down dappled and rich; on the leaf-mould paths a mazed shuffling of lilac coins. In the beech part of the wood there is a stillness, prelude to the torrid summer noon, as if all life hushes to the risping of grasshoppers in the nearby meadow, and the sweet regular call of the cuckoo which brings a fire of joy into my heart.

The honeysuckle at this time holds its embryonic flowers: the tiny red-tinged clubs, like the horns of a young deer, which will eventually become the scrolled corollas, at whose lips the night-moths feed.

The tubes lengthen steadily until in early June they are slender fingers with swollen apple-tinged tips. The sun ripens them until they split, and the lips curl back, and the stamens protrude with their load of pollen. Now the scent, created by the secretion of honey at the base of the corolla, is broadcast upon the still air.

Only perhaps in music has been written fully the summer evening, whose glory is in the sun-sweet woodbine spreading fragrance, and the fiery spirit of the swifts on high as the sky darkens. Much of it is taken secretly to my heart, fruit of a thousand wanderings under bright Vega and the early stars, and has become inexpressible, being a part of my existence. It is one of those matters in which there is not so much thought as intangible feeling. You say 'honeysuckle' – a word only – and I see ivory virgin lips at dusk, the many carven clusters against the sky, I smell the fragrance and feel around me the dark secret earth which bears so many sweet things. Chafers boom among the full-foliaged trees; the western sky is green and night is in the east. Here I hang between sun and star in the hour of transition, a calm hopelessness of beauty upon me like the last sustained chords of *In a Summer Garden*, created by Delius, that wracked egocentric genius who put all of earth's wonder and human sadness into music.

THE IMAGINATION TO THE WRAITH

I am sitting by your sea of a generation ago, having come to a time when I feel myself to be unified with you.

There have been times when in arrogant orthodoxy I have denied you, though that was seldom. But more numerous have been the times when I questioned the reality or application of your idealism. Now that I have come naturally into the track of your way of thinking I have no need of self-questioning or introversion. To-night you and I are one, sun and sea bind me to you as night upon the earth.

It came at the time of sun-in-the-sands. I am apart and unfriended as you were, walking by your sea of Devon and Folkestone, feeling you to be living in me.

Your sea: the eternal thunderous energy, manifested in the rush and pebbly surge and underdrag you watched, patrolled by the gulls you loved. This is in its fundamentals yours, the conception and spirit of it, the deep inspiration, and only the present pigment of fact is mine, your brain being dust and your eyes sightless. I see for you the sun thrown back in a brilliant sheen by the ruddy grains of sand: mine are the pearly scalloped shells and wine-stained pebbles whose round smoothness is a story of sea-life: herring-gulls aslant the breeze, the white blown sky of sunset like smoke over the town, the dark old rocks cluttering the shore. The people on the front − I think of the Leas − are of your time as of mine.

All these things you know and gave me, and to-night I understand the nature of the gift genuinely, instead of by assumption. I can never hope to attain the meticulous vision of your mind when confronted by cosmic beauty, but there is much I can learn.

They pass, the timeless vacant faces; who shall say there is no Evelyn, no dream-flax among them?

The sun is dying. Oh, Maddison, your sea speaks to me. ...[1]

(*Spring, Torquay, 1942*)

* * * * *

[1] Willie Maddison, drowned at the end of Henry Williamson's *The Pathway*.

41

The poor old padre is trying very hard to convert me. I don't know whether I look young and easy to influence, but a number of other people have expressed agnostic views to him and he has just left them: but he is concentrating hard on me! I have had one or two very nice chats with him, but have never got down to fundamental arguments because he is so busy. I have told him that I am not a nihilist, but have my own personal type of religion and he is very tolerant, but I know he feels responsibility for me; and I tell him not to feel he's responsible. The main fact which emerges is that he is a thoroughly decent and Christian fellow − I doubt if there is a better padre anywhere − and heightens my belief in Christ's principles, which is my very reason for disagreeing with modern religion, the Church and most professing Christians. So that's where we stick.

I must make up all the lee-way in my writing one day. This life, being one which is fundamentally and physically good (which agrees with my ideas), is therefore rather hard on the imaginative tissues: but I feel I am not losing myself, merely allowing part of myself to become dormant, ready to flare up at the right time. I always was two types of person to some extent − one of whom lies in a field and the other flies night-fighters (or hopes to!) − so it's not a new job to let one person go to sleep.

* * * * *

5 April 1942

We were issued with flying kit do-day. It's beautiful equipment, worth about £80 in all, and when I saw that wonderfully made stuff, with silk gloves, etc. (50*s*. per pair), I decided one need never be at a loss for an argument against a clothing coupon wangler. Clothes rationing *is* justified, because there is a vast amount of very high quality stuff needed for flying suits especially. The gloves consist of one pair of silk ones, then a pair of woollen, then leather gauntlets on top.

A letter from mother contained the phrase, 'Almond blossom, palm willow, jasmine and daffodils ... home is full of flowers.' Gosh, what I'm going to make up for after the war! That just represents Easter as it should be, and here am I missing it. I like to think of my woods, and all the stages I used to watch − right through to high summer, with such great interest. It seems funny to think of it all going ahead without me, but I feel it has something of my thought in it now. I suppose that's my faith, really. It means that wherever I am there are the same stars and the same living things, all of which are familiar, so that the mere face of the locality is relatively non-important.

11 April 1942

This afternoon I monopolized the wireless in the Squadron Recreation Room, which normally churns out dance music at all times of the day and night, in order to hear the Delius Violin Concerto in the Orchestral Concert. Actually there were very few people there, and I was ensconced right by the wireless with a determined feeling not to be done out of it, so just for once I had *my* choice! A chap came up after a few minutes and peered at the knobs: then he said, 'Is this the Forces programme?' and I replied, 'No, the Home Service,' as if quite unable to understand what he was getting at. Then he continued, 'This is beginning to get irksome, isn't it?' to which I replied sweetly, 'Is it?' The poor devil wandered off miserably. Actually with the high average type here we have several good-music-lovers, and we sometimes manage to keep the morons at bay. Anyway the music was simply lovely and it was a real tonic to hear it again: it seems to bring out a different part of oneself. It is definitely the most beautiful violin concerto I have ever heard. Of course it is specialized like all Delius, that strange personal poetry with which I just happen to be lucky enough to be in tune.

* * * * *

On leave, Spring 1942

When the farewells were said we went out together with a feeling of deep sadness into the orchard. At first the blackness was intense and we blundered from tree to tree, trying to find the path which led to the river. It was no use yet. I stood holding a grazed hand, as if in a trance, suddenly knowing clearly what was going to happen to my friend. It was a good decision, to wait until we were used to the dark. When one stands waiting at night, and there is no obligation to speak, thoughts crowd thickly to the imagination, every one huge and clear-cut so that one is thrilled with the revelations they bring.

I stood dead quiet, breathing through my mouth. Two feet away the dim shape of Don faced me, also breathing as if slyly stealing the air, waiting. In suspension of all activity we behaved identically. Thought flowed between us in silence. Each wondered how much the other saw of the inevitable.

The stars glimmered into my vision, winking in the sky near-clouded with blossom. A slight wind made the stars shiver and wince, and some petals fell soundlessly past us. When it was still again we could see quite well the elbowed apple-trunks rising about us from the dimness of the grass. About our heads swam a pallor of blossom and the air was loaded with its icy sweetness. Through gaps we could see the quiet reigning stars.

We stood together while one loosed petal after another went down to its rest in the grass, seeing that all our life's friendship was being gathered into this charged atmosphere. This night, these stars, the blossom covering the quiet miles of our country.

* * * * *

Eastbourne, 12 May 1942
I went away on leave at the right time. The poor blighters who were left, getting ready for King and Queen's visit, had P.T. and drill for pretty well the whole week. On the first day they had four hours' non-stop P.T. and over fifty reported sick at once with sunburn and minor sunstroke. There are stories of cadets who were delirious in their sleep. This apparently went on throughout the whole week. Everyone was brassed off: the whole course has been held up a week, and now they have got to make up by working in the evenings and on Saturday afternoon.

We who were for Eastbourne left Elfordleigh and marched to the station in pouring rain, full kit, 50 per cent of the Flight drunk. We got on a special troop-train at about 10.45, and tried to get to sleep soon after we left. There were six to a carriage, and we made sardine arrangements to get our feet up. When I awoke from a doze I was very uncomfortable and couldn't move. We had our greatcoats over us, but sleep was difficult because we were really just sitting, and it was impossible to get our heads down. I awoke at one time and we had halted in a station − I shall never know where. At last we awoke again to find we were just moving off. I slept again − we were by now sprawled in weird attitudes like a battlefield scene.

I woke up at about five, feeling I had had enough sleep. It was just beginning to get light so I went and watched the dawn come up from the corridor − I alone in that whole train, with all the pale faces like corpses − terrible amount of condensed moisture − in the compartments strewn around with greatcoats, legs, arms, etc., etc. Very dramatic! They all missed something too. I felt really good there on my own: it turned out we were still in the West Country (we ran into Yeovil at about 5.30) and the dawn after all that rain was lovely. I have never seen it that way before − the smoke from our engine hanging in coils over the fields which were dark blue-green, cows still settled in their night attitudes, dim woods, a low vapour over the fields, flashes of streams passing by where they caught the lemon of the small patch of clear sky over the hills: quiet farms, not yet milking (what a triumph to see the world even before the farmer). Later there was a blue-green purity about everything, and when we slowed down I could hear blackbirds shouting their joy ...

I am writing this in the Grand Hotel, and it certainly is that: vast, with miles of corridors: a whole Wing is here. We are about twenty yards from the sea this time, but unfortunately I have not got a sea view. I bagged a room on my own. I am very pleased with this: it gives one a certain amount of that almost non-existent thing, peace and quiet. I should be able to swot nicely up here later on. One thing: I am glad to live in an atmosphere which is not crowded with obscenities. This room has a mirror, a basin, windows which I can open at night, hooks on the door, a radiator which I don't use; the beds are the standard type, but larger, so that even I can lie fully stretched out and not touch the bottom end.

The bathroom is right next door, and has a superb bath which I sampled last night. We really do very well indeed.

THE BELOVED

When I am in the fields she lies
Alone upon the hills, for she is Day
And I am Night, and brighest shine her eyes
When I must look away.
But briefly as in summer dawn we meet,
Her beauty in a flood
Burns vagrant through my blood.

And when the swift floats high
On molten tide of sunset, silently
Together in the meadows do we lie,
But never wed shall be:
For soon she sleeps in mist and I must rise,
And when the stars are grown
Must seek the hills alone.

(*Eastbourne 1942*)[1]

SONNET: PARTHENOGENESIS[2]

Strange, the unpatterned riot of these years;
A trackless garden bright with ruin, sown
With pale enthusiasms and fed with tears
And flowered of joy, the blossom soonest blown.
I have sought much, pursued the ancient stars
And lusted after spiritual gold;
Drunk colour to the day's end; found in wars
My naked soul drinks deeply, I behold
A finer surge of life. And I have run
And tried to laugh, and fancied I have been
To hell and heaven, journeyed with the sun.
But late I have unlearned all that I've seen
In my wracked garden, and found it growing fair
And everlasting summer biding there.

(*On leave, Summer 1942*)

THE WIND

As I think of those springs when the breeze
Whispered me
Through the susurrant trees,
Stirred the flowers of the mind —
All I hear is the wind.

The swallow forgets in the height
Of the sky,
And the eyes of the night
Passing golden away
Salute only the day.

---

[1] Cf. Williamson: 'James Farrar sought the hills alone during his life (he was 18 when he wrote the above), but perhaps now he has found and wed the Beloved.' (Letter to an unidentified Devon newspaper, mid-1950s).

[2] See *White Paper*, p. 56 § 3.

46

I have broken my faith, I am tired,
But the wind
Seeks the unopened blossom, the fancy unfired,
Stirring ash in my brain
That will glow not again.

(*Eastbourne 1942*)

OLD AGE

Having read,
Alone sits Age,
Life open at
The final page,

And seeks again
The words before −
But they are lost
For evermore:

For each page turned
Is turned to stone,
And now remains
The last alone;

Till that which made
Of youth a flower
Shall close the book
And strike the hour.

(*Eastbourne 1942*)

The march up to Crosby House under the rim of the Downs − a skyline pulsing with golden gorse under the heat-whitened sky. The Downs, attained once a week in a labouring uphill run, are swept by the pure winds that die, clogged with fragrance, in bowls lined with the sloping gorse, above which the sun stands pitiless, giving no shade: nothing seems to live on those Downs, except the grasshoppers flipping across a background of murmurous whisperings which are insect-sunworship: the tiny white figures of runners conquering the skyline: and, of course, the butterflies, vividly trembling from grass to grass, red and blue and black-dusty wings a-quiver about one's recumbent form.

On the Downs it is possible to lie nearly naked, to lie alone with summer, whose sweetness blesses the white flesh truant from our civilization.

Four times a day we march along the road drowsy with heat, with houses sunken among their still, coloured trees. Tar on the road is soft, so that we march with dull thudding steps. Sweat trembles above our eyes and soaks our bodies. We march with steel helmets on our left shoulders, against the sometime menace of that white-heat sky, and we pass lines of tanks parked, at the rutted edge of the road, huge slumbrous things under their awnings of camouflage netting. Sometimes their crews, resting by scattered parts of the tanks, watch us with the ingenuous eyes of children in the sun. Something of the summer pervades the spirits of all of us, making us slow and quiescent, honey-sweet in thought when our way of life permits. For we work hard, and sweat, and only after the evening's study can one relax until sunset.

Then I walk many times along the promenade. By this time of day in summer one senses peace lying horizontally in a thin golden light: no more the earth-smiting vibrance of perpendicular sunlight, suffocating one between layers of harsh light and dust. The sea lies sweetly calm and the distant pier ripples with golden kindness at low tide. Gulls walk gravely like snow at the sea's edge.

* * * * *

I had no difficulty in getting myself on the list for running. We were away a little after two and as very few of us were interested in running except as a means of reaching the café on the Downs we made an easy pace. I was a little impatient, though, and was glad to break away as we left the road where it broadened into the first chalk slope of the Downs. I broke away round the hill-curve to the left and then continued parallel to my original route with the brow between me and my fellows. As I climbed the noise of traffic and voices seemed to fall away from me and there was only the heat-blue breast of the hill ahead of me, streaked with flames of gorse, and the silence of the sky all about. Occasionally a short burst of larksong chipped the silence, or a drifting of air − less than a breeze − reminded me of the drowsy hush of the sea which lay spread on my left. At such moments the grass rippled dusty-bright in the sun and the heads of harebells quivered gently and were still again. There were many flowers on the Downs, especially in the lush grass in the lee of the gorse bushes.

The hills floated in ethereal beauty, haze-blue, rising out of a sea of heat. The hollows were vast dust-bowls of silence, drugged with scent. I lay all afternoon on a slope licked with gorse-flames as far as the eye could see, feeling the wind's spasmodic breath as a tingling chill on my heated flesh. The sky pulsed blue-white, and nothing moved beneath it save the vivid-winged butterflies of summer flickering from flower to grass, and the dry-voiced grasshoppers that I heard all around but never saw; occasionally there were the far-off voices of the runners passing over the skyline, empty like voices in a dream.

The sun burned the hills into dragonfly brilliance, flowers bright and vain lapping the sky's edge.

* * * * *

31 May 1942
The thick-starred nights of summer are probed only by distant searchlights.

I am sitting in the NAAFI having a morning guzzle to restore my health and strength after the strenuous business of getting up at 8 o'clock. What a lovely day Sunday is here. No making of beds if you don't feel like it, leisurely breakfast, stroll to get a paper. But here a sterner note creeps in. I have developed a conscience about my domestic jobs. I swore I would jettison all sweeping, etc., for to-day and sit right down and write. But I couldn't do it. There was a thousandth of an inch of dust on my wash-basin, and I saw two hairs on the floor, so before I could stop myself I had folded my blankets – roughly, the only holiday note – swept the floor, scrubbed the basin, cleaned the mirror, and even cleaned the windows which needed doing badly. All this is a record of how the Air Force makes susceptible people hygiene-conscious. I think it's a very good influence really, although it's very trying to have a conscience.

I discovered a starling's nest this morning in a cranny in the stone balustrade, only a few feet from my window, so I am looking forward to quite an interesting time watching the youngsters being fed. I wish I had my binoculars, even at this range of about a dozen feet, because they enlarge three diameters and would facilitate really good observation.

* * * * *

We are getting well into the work now. It takes some handling, but thanks to the private study, which really is necessary, I think I am getting it O.K. Some parts are extremely interesting, such as the theory of Astro, which is partly my old friend Astronomy, and includes the fascinating business of knowing the stars; and Meteorology, useful in any walk of life, and pleasing to the naturalist because of the study of cloud-forms, which we are now approaching. Clouds and the stars are things I never quite managed to study properly in Civvy Street, so I enjoy being *forced* to do so in this syllabus in RAF time!

* * * * *

We were turned out of bed three times on Friday night by the alarm bells. After the second I had just laboriously come back, dumped my tin hat and respirator, taken off my greatcoat, folded it in the approved style to save time in the morning, relieved myself of my boots, hung up my tunic, taken off my socks, placed my trousers under the bed, got into bed with a feeling of 'Ah, now for some sleep' – and lay there for precisely thirty seconds before the alarms went off again.

* * * * *

I walked down to the general billiard-cum-notice-board-cum-wireless room last Sunday afternoon, and a wave of Elgar transfixed me at the doorway. All other inhabitants had apparently been driven out by the Sunday Orchestral Concert; and I joined the small gathering of good-music-lovers one always finds somewhere in a community like this: a lot of statues round the wireless; not an eyelid moved, not a word was spoken. It was the *Enigma Variations*. How I enjoyed those few minutes.

* * * * *

Early June 1942
In the evening, when that perfect day drew on to its perfection of honey-light, I sat, cool at last, with Don and his girl Jean in the garden of the 'Woolpack' at Banstead. How good it was to talk quietly, amicably, with my oldest and best friend, feeling that we had at last bridged the

gap caused by our development in different directions. Then, we went apart because we were no longer identical in outlook: now, after a couple of years, I had caught up – I had learnt what he probably knew in the first place, that lack of identity in outlook is no bar, and is, in fact, the spice of friendship. We were now complementary, and yet in many ways still equal.

How good to watch people drinking, talking, moving about and sampling the scent of the large dog-roses which were profuse along the hedge: to drink clear ale with the enthusiasm of real thirst after the day's heat: to study Jean, whom I like and who has considerable charm and not a little beauty in spite of the excessive make-up of our generation. I got on well with her because she evidently liked me. I found myself talking easily, an art newly learnt as far as girls were concerned: getting head above water after that terrible tendency to parched-mouthed inarticulation between the ages of sixteen and eighteen. I remember feeling inordinately pleased with life. Her eyes, with the purity which is their great asset, were lovely as the sky now green with after-sunset. How grand to be just a little grown-up, to sit and admire, and talk sanely and afterwards making nothing of it! So we sat and talked until the garden was a lake of shadow from hedge to hedge, and the perfume of the dog-roses hung on the air about us, and still the cuckoo called, clear and regular, across the gardens. Coolness, friendship, laughter – what more can one ask of a summer evening?

*   *   *   *   *

Long purple curved shadow of bandstand on shingle beach. Large greyish stones nearby, smaller and strewn with dried black seaweed to high-water-mark shelf of shingle. Below, sparser sand-and-shingle scours, running out to marks of receding tide like hair-tresses printed on finely stone-dotted sand.

White gull on weed-green breakwater.

Beyond, wet sand: same colour as sea and sky. Sea coming in like millpond, quiet ripples brimming in to turn in widening lip when already running up sand, runs in until force gone, pure water disappears where brilliant white gulls stand. Ripples seem to come in from sky, quiet grey sunlight haze, no horizon, all pale light.

Pier building remote, pearly in sunshine, long reflection gleaming down shallow water, blurred pale shell-coloured by incoming ripples, same on wet sand.

* * * * *

The nearest Bofors gun is just above the beach, twenty-five yards away. Twenty-five yards is not far, and every time the gun fired with that peculiarly vicious staccato bark it seemed that the hotel was being struck by five bombs in quick succession. When I got ouside people were running across the road and shouting in amazement as the flights of tracer shells rose like strings of rubies into the starry sky. Above the town the pallid glare of incendiaries blossomed pink once, twice, three times as further H.E.s fell. Fiercer into the sky mounted the magnesium light, till the reflected glare rode in every window.

Once more the throb of engines as the last raider came back, fairly low, making his getaway. Smack, smack, smack, smack, smack, five more startled firebirds rose in line to meet another string ascending from beyond Crosby House. A swifter succession of tracers soared up from the direction of the pier. Other guns joined in. From all directions strings of red globes sailed up into the sky to intersect at a point directly above us. But the aircraft droned safely away to sea.

CLOUDY DAWN (STATION DEFENCE)

At the top of the tower we emerged into a pale radiance of moonfire. We spoke in low voices with the two we were relieving, while looking for the first time at the silent town below. The summer air was calm down there, hung with thick flower-scents like patches of colour on a sea-surface, but at this height the wind whirled fine sand at us from the decayed sandbags and the quietness was broken by the slap of cord against flagpole.

The first two departed. Our main problem was to get out of the wind, so we settled under the lee of the sandbag wall, looking at the dark blur of town roofs, the sea's molten brilliance and the wind-blown night sky. The waves along the deserted, mined beaches hissed loudly. At times the wind made moan through the body of the moon-silvered

Vickers machine-gun hanging muzzle to sky before us on its tall tripod. I got up to check the gun, finding real joy in its silken efficiency, smooth slide of breech block and click home of magazine with its rattling pregnancy of rounds. My first experience of a serviceable gun.

Blake's words came to me on the wind as I sat down again on the spare gun-case:

> The moon, like a flower
> In heaven's high bower,
> Sits with silent delight
> And smiles on the night.

and I smiled to myself. What pleasure there is in this habit of recalling, and creating one's own world of imagination: words and sights and sounds known of old to the mind, unheard during the factual progress of the day's work, but cast up again like trembling sea-foam on the shores of night. Wind on a high tower, the hissing sea, silent sky trailing its shadows over the slopes of the Downs and across the town and into the flat distances of coastline. More recordings on the sound-track of memory, perhaps to revive in some future reveries.

We made up the log-book entry: 'Q45. $\frac{5}{10}$ St. & Sc. Visibility excellent, fresh SW. breeze,' which is a moonlit night reduced to pencil and paper.

Quiet conversation ensued, with long silences. The moon faded, becoming like the face of a drowning maiden under tresses of wandering cloud, sinking to obscurity. My companion looked away into the darkness, his dark lank hair lifting in the wind, as he sought a cigarette. His face was ruddy for a moment, then the match hissed away downwind.

We sat in silence. The tip of his cigarette fumed and wasted in brightness against the dark. Once more the moon smiled upon us, hung spinning a misty web behind growing cloud, and was gone. Low stratus cloud was coming off the Downs, but there was pallor in the north-east.

Soon after a blue-green fissure appeared at the horizon, bounded by smoky lenticular cloud like charred wrecks of Zeppelins. Slow trails of cloud crept across the gap, behind the etched outline of a nearby church steeple. The colour behind the spire became pale sea-green, and for a moment there appeared a bead of pure silver, shining out from under the roof of the rift.

For a minute and a half the morning star hung steady beneath the eaves of heaven before a tarry caterpillar of cloud stole across its brilliance. Soon a dim red bank appeared lower, on the horizon, and the upper rift, narrowing slightly, shone purer, and I became aware of a faint distinctness in my surroundings.

A distant bell sang the three-quarter. A minute later came the boom from the nearby steeple, now standing against a long streak of primrose-green which faded to a mauve haze and thus to darkness over the sea. A slight warmth now in the notched edges of the rift, but still the northern end was nightbound, like marble. Several notes of blackbird song were heard against the 'hush-hush' of sea on shore. Silence, and pallor over the town, blue-dusked like a Dulac picture, set at the foot of slumbering Downs with their iron-coloured sky, and beyond, vast galleons of cumulus riding like icebergs in the deathly sea-sky. I shivered in the dawn wind.

Then from dewy lawn and roof-ridge of Eastbourne sang out a massed chorus of purity, day-song of blackbirds. I could see golden straws of light scattered on a wave-crest, gathering and clashing apart in a million drops, rising from troughs and leaping again in spray, like the harps in the opening of the second suite from Ravel's *Daphnis and Chloë*. Light leaping from a shadowed sea, and the clear music of harps, is in the dawn-song of blackbirds.[1]

Many puffs and trails of tarry clouds now hung along the yellowing sky-gleam, as distinctness came to our sandbagged shelter, the mast and stay-wires cutting our skyline, and the roofs beneath. The over-rift sky was beginning to glow, a pale radiance spreading to bases of individual clouds, and the back-cloth of layer cloud darkly luminous with a promise of Turner colours.

At this time I went down to the foot of the tower to act as runner, privately to wander in the gardens. There were red ramblers in bloom all along the stone walls: sun-dried lawns, a shingle drive lined with dark cuprous trees, and a lodge with a greenhouse and, as might be expected, honeysuckle. I went down a little overgrown path to a hollow

---

[1] Look at the orchestral score of the *Daphnis and Chloë* dawn-scene and you'll *see* the 'million drops!' The music actually *looks* like a pointilliste canvas. When on leave, in the summer of 1943, Jim went to book his ticket for a Ravel chamber-music concert at the Wigmore Hall. He found the door open and the pianist practising, went in and stood spellbound, engulfed by the giant virtuoso waves of sound (enhanced by the emptiness of the hall) of *Jeux d'Eau*.

under tall trees. There were signs of earlier beauty in spite of the recent neglect, vouched for by spur-valerian, yellow flags, scabious and red-velvet and smooth-mauve antirrhinums growing at will amongst gipsy campions, daisies and yellow trefoils in ivy-choked beds. In the centre, well shaded by trees, I came across a tiny lawn speckled with closed daisies, having a bird-splashed sundial on a chipped stone pillar scarred with gold lichens and moss. The battered face of the sundial looked very old, and was corroded green, and I felt strangely out of time, and away from life, in this half-lost garden where there was no sound but the throbbing and cooing of doves in the still trees. Huge ferns grew against a low wall dividing this from a darker hollow, in which I could see nothing. I found an old seat, beneath which a wild violet grew, and sat there for some time. I felt I had come a long way from the Air Force and machine-guns.

(Eastbourne, Summer 1942)

WHITE PAPER[1]

Lying on a slope of the Downs above Eastbourne on a golden late summer afternoon one month before my nineteenth birthday, I began to conceive a new personal idealism through which I hope to revise my attitude to the world around me. It followed on the heels of a slightly disturbing feeling of purposelessness which I have known several times lately, due in some degree, perhaps, to the inactivity of our present life: but not entirely. Sometimes, engaged upon a train of thought, I imagine I glimpse for a briefest instant a rift beneath the veneer of culture and abstruse thought on which our rank as *Homo Sapiens*, the Highest, depends. And seeing this void I have felt even the faint stirrings of primeval terror. It is like experiencing an air raid in the house you have inhabited all your life, the solid eternal house in which you were born: you realize then, suddenly, how fragile the whole structure *could be* if conditions were to change, if by chance a bomb should strike it. As things are, everything is sound: the unknown is the void. So of our life I have felt in brief revelations the naked truth that we are walking

---

[1] First published in *Leaves in the Storm* (London 1947, ed. Stefan Schimanski and Henry Treece), a collection of excerpts from war diaries.

upon rafters above emptiness, rafters whose strength is of our own making, whose thickness depends on the extent of our determination to fashion our spirits in greatness so that they can look upon the universe with equanimity. I have not fashioned, I have wandered with the adze in my hand, preferring a reasonably rational epicurism, spiritually and otherwise: my only desire, apart from a few pale assimilated ideals, being that the five senses and the 'inward eye,' or spiritual perception, should continue to be laved with pleasurable impressions.

No longer do I wish to be as one of the glistening wheels of thistle-down which rolled on trackless air above the hillside. To be suspended in beauty in the gaze of the sun − yes: but what of the skittish dance at every breath of thyme-laden wind, the long helpless journey into the valley's void, the ultimate crucifixion against grass tufts or the black spiny arms of furze? Rather should I be as the plant that looses them, growing steadfast on its grassy slope, aspiring to the sun in summer, sere in the wind's tune in winter, reborn in spring. Where before I have been governed by whim, henceforth must I be governed by resolve ...

This is to be a record of that self-forged metamorphosis. I consider it important because this is the first time when an ideal of some stature has arisen independently within myself, and if influenced, at least not fostered by an outside source. Having been led, sometimes well, sometimes ill, since the awakening of my life, I am now, towards the end of the decade, making some effort to take the helm myself. I am not claiming to plan a vast reversal of habits and life-intentions − such changes, even if possible, would probably be harmful. Rather am I trying to develop the core of myself, upward and away from the girdle of acquired habitualism and small-scale thinking, so that any desirable assets attached thereto shall aspire upwards with me and the rest fall away.

This desire for what I can only call, in the steps of a writer whose constant influence I must acknowledge, parthenogenesis, was conceived through an emotion of fullness and tranquillity as I lay on the baked August turf. The impersonal benediction of sunlight, the satisfaction I felt in the loneliness of the Downs, and the realisation that I could draw my life-force wholly from such loneliness, that it should be greater and purer in application to my fellow-beings, became fused into a desire to live always thus in equipoise with humanity as with the earth itself. My lack of constructiveness, I felt, would be brought to an end as I developed the idea of learning breadth and independence of thought from Nature, applying the new freemindedness to the understanding of man, learning to enjoy myself not artificially, a little viciously, a little desperately, which is the dubious gift of our civilization, but spontaneously, deeply, through the enlargement of my sympathies and the growth of the latent pleasure I have always found in the humanness of humanity.

I considered my friends, the particular ambitions of some of them, trying to create a parallel according to my own interests. What I decided was governed by my long-held opinion that an individual is only justifying himself fully if he is doing the work towards which he has an inclination, to which he is best suited. In this way not only is the work done better, but its accomplishment gives rise to the maximum feeling of creative achievement. And I think that a man is forced to be half-empty if he is forced to spend his waking energies on what is not, for him, creation. The thought of writers who must be clerks, of potential athletes who must be navvies, of clerks who must sell matches, is not an inspiring one. All this jamming of square pegs into round holes is governed by the necessity to get bread. I must get bread, and at least for a considerable time it is not conceivable that I shall get bread through holding what I consider to be the right opinions on how to live life. Therefore I shall do the other man's work, with sufficient enthusiasm to supply me with the necessities to continue living. But always I shall be, not the labourer, the clerk, the sailor, the tramp, but the idealist, and never shall I willingly stay in one rut of meniality long enough for the force to be crushed. I have a friend whose life-interest is biochemistry; and he is an efficient biochemist. He is a whole man, because he is fulfilled. I am one who loves life, who would create through understanding. Therefore my true trade shall be as a liver of live, an understander, a conceiver.

Such was my decision. It entailed work. I must acquire knowledge, just as every man must acquire knowledge, for my trade: besides learning everything possible from what is held before the retina or my eye, I must also seek actively in other ways, by widening my appreciation in such spheres as literature and music, in order that I may rectify personal shortcomings and succeed as far as possible in removing any trace of a beam from my own eye by acquaintance with the minds and visions of others. To become erudite while remaining a spiritual Adam;

to take to myself the greatest cosmic truth and the least significance of contact, comradeship and love — these are my ideals. And further, having learned to re-create in writing whose soundness must be guaranteed by the basing of my sense of values not on transient enthusiasms, but on one constant level of belief, a belief founded on naturalness which will not wax and wane with the aberrations of that semi-denaturalized child of nature, mankind. I am of mankind and subject to the wildest aberrations, like a spirit-level tipped this way and that; but my belief must by its constancy be the bubble that tells me which way and how far I am tipping.

This nature-root I regard as the basis of my resolve, but it is not an end in itself. It is to mould me for the fullest and least bigoted receptiveness to the voices of man, sky and earth. Perhaps the whole idea is best epitomized by the use of the term 'primal sanities.'

This is in no sense to be a philosophy of puritan insularity, which only too popularly is held to be an intrinsic part of idealism. It is my fullest intention to behave as normal flesh and blood — that is the first primal sanity learned from Nature — yet, as far as possible, flesh and blood that has some idea what it is doing. Most of us succeed at one time in acting well according to the dictates of the brain, at another time according to the heart. Often, as in a happy marriage, the two are cultivated so as to be complementary. Sometimes, on the other hand, they are unnecessarily at variance. Occasionally, under these conditions, it will occur that the two cannot continue to act independently, and the attempted reconciliation, or the reconciliation of one or both to the environment, is what is known as disillusionment. In Eden perhaps we could leave the brain to look after itself, and the heart may well be forgotten in an intellectual Utopia: but this is human life, which comprises physical Eden and celibate intellectualism and every stage and variation between the two, and which, ideally, demands the ability to walk with surety in every sphere. The vital point is that I *must* walk in every sphere, some of the ways of which compare unfavourably with a tightrope. Therefore must I look to my equilibrium. Harmony of the mental and physical planes, eventual experience of all human joys and sorrows without warping excess in any, must be welded to form my balancing-rod.

* * * * *

From a letter to his Mother, June 21 1942
I got my dinner after a 150-yard queue to-day − out of the dining hall, across the main hall, through the recreation room, along a corridor, up two flights of stairs and along another corridor. And when I say 'room' I mean a large one, for the Grand is a spacious place.

Queueing is a thing you never escape in the RAF. If it's not for meals it's the same for the NAAFI. This is not a grouse because it's unavoidable: but I would just like some of the Mr. T's and Mrs. B's to try it; not only when they are sweating with marching and very hungry, but when they only have half an hour in which to get through that queue, have a meal, clean up boots and buttons and get out on parade again ready for the afternoon's work − 1.30 to 5.30. After-dinner nap − oh yes! I might make them think just a tiny bit whether they *are* doing anything, or making any sacrifices. For that matter I would like them to do any of the things we do, just as an eye-opener. I have no grouses at any personal discomfort or inconvenience as such, it is merely *comparative* sacrifice which makes me writhe. I don't mind going to the ends of the earth to be killed if only I can think that the B's and T's of the civilian world are being shaken out of their armchair minds, and toddling a few steps themselves ...

I am writing in the Oak Cabin, my expensive haunt, in the middle of the most wonderful meal I have had for weeks. I ordered myself to come here, as usual purely for the sake of eating decent food in a decent atmosphere. Sausage (and *not* beef) and bacon (that *bends* when you put your knife in it − juicy!) and mashed potatoes (without dull lumps in it!) and *new* bread and butter and *coffee* and a tablecloth!!!!!! (just letting off steam, I can't restrain myself) ...

From a letter to his Mother, 17 July 1942
It is exactly a year ago that I went to Croydon to join up. It seems longer than that since I was really a civilian, not even an AC2 on deferred service. I wonder if civilians realize exactly what rights and privileges they have, that is, the ones who aren't so town-bound as to cage themselves in self-made taboos and restrictions. I must admit I shall be glad when I once more have the chance to order my own life, go where I please when I please, insult a man I dislike, regardless of his position, and not be ordered about and treated as dirt by people with less than a fifth of even my limited intelligence. That is the one thing

about the Services which any reasonable human being could object to. In wartime I don't mind: the whole thing is a wonderful experience and I wouldn't be out of it for anything: it probably develops you as fast as anything in life could, and that's what I want. But I have a feeling that after the war I shall not slip back into ordinary life as easily as I have occasionally thought (in the intervals of vowing to be a tramp!). I have learnt what a kick I can get out of breaking away from smooth secure life, and that I am honestly happier and have a real sense of achievement when up against difficulties. Not responsibilities, because responsibilities tie me to other people, limiting my actions and making me feel like an old man, but genuine personal difficulties which it is my pleasure by brain or spirit to overcome. It is a thing too often said, but I find (or will find, when my life is broad enough to admit of things of such scale) that only in difficulties does one discover one's true inner strength. And that once a thing is acquired there is less pleasure in the having than in the effort to acquire. Ready-made thoughts, of course, but then I can't afford to be a philosopher because I am a U/T[1] Observer-Radio. Well, the point of all this is the change of my reason for not wanting to fall in line after the war. Previously I just felt there was nothing in civvy life to suit my particular bent, if any, and that I would rather 'mess around' and hope for the best. Now I have by no means completed my self-searchings, but I am developing a theory that I can find something more tangible by breaking away, something which is not concerned with money or standard of living, but with one's real self, which is a less ephemeral thing. I know that when I settle down and things run in an orderly way, as has happened before now, I feel completely ordinary, with no talents, and no desires beyond those of my neighbour. That is mediocrity which I hate, and there is a spiritual traffic jam inside me. But if I can live apart, even dangerously, making my own decisions and relying on myself for their success, then I am enjoying life twenty times more.

This, which used to be a romanticized Williamson-fostered boy's dream, is changing into a very real feeling. I want to be able to stand apart and watch people and use life, instead of being used by it, which is the tragic story of so many people in the suburbs. And this is not easy, as I can imagine. I couldn't have tried it if I had not gone into

---

[1] 'Under Training'.

the Forces, but I think this is going to make me able to take knocks if anything is. I will say right now that I have no consideration for social status and normal standards of success, because I don't think they mean much. It's quite possible that for a number of years, or even all time, certain people will not be able to think of me without calling me a failure because I shall not have a 'house,' a car and so on. This doesn't mean that I intend to ruin my life, because I don't. The picture is this: in an ordinary job I can get a living and even advancement if my youth dies enough for me to raise enthusiasm for it, and I shall live like a codfish. If I try my own hand I may or may not get a living, and I shall live alternately like a rainbow-fish and a dolorous deep-sea whale, but I may get a kick out of it …

It's funny, you know, how I seem to affect various people differently. Some people seem to find me very likeable, and others just can't think up scathing enough words for me. It's a curious business, not many people sit on the fence and consider me just as an 'ordinary chap'; they seem to like the two extremes − either they think quite a lot of me (as I flatter myself one or two people do) or else they think I am a twirp, a pansy and anything else that comes into their self-opinionated heads. I wish I could see myself from the outside, and try to understand their point of view, if it can be understood.

We are doing nothing but mess around still, and I am having a chance to organize myself for spare evenings. Whereas previously I had no ideas beyond burying myself at the pictures, I am now forcing myself to make my own amusement: it's very good mental exercise to get out of the rut like that, because when you only want to go to the pictures it means your perception and interest in life has got a bit rusty at the edges. I now thoroughly enjoy myself by walking aimlessly round the place, staring hard and long at everything and receiving impressions. I go on the front and watch the sea for half an hour on end, until I start really thinking, and suddenly realize the significance of what I am looking at. This may sound crazy to you, but it is mentally like a luxurious hot bath: my old friend, the process of taking the wrinkles out of the mind. I am hoping to do some writing in a day or two, but I shan't be able to work up anything with real form.

A lot of the boys are having a beer-up to-night to celebrate the departure of the Straight Observers, or rather to have a farewell party. Little Jimmy still sticks to his word and is not getting beered up on any extra occasions. Once per course is enough for me, the night-before-posting celebration when everyone joins in. I have been coaxed to-night, but am not having any: I am convinced that by keeping up this rigorous refusal at all other times I am as near a T.T. as I can be, while nevertheless enjoying a very occasional good time. This doesn't sound too bad to you, does it? One beer-up in three months doesn't do anyone any harm, but it's the habit that is the thing to watch against, as in smoking, and I'm not getting caught.

* * * * *

Every week we have a special spit-and-polish parade, four chosen Flights, and the C.O. has a snoop round. Yesterday the Wing Commander turned up and instead of all four Flights being inspected simultaneously by the Flight Commanders, one of whom the C.O. may accompany, the Wing Commander decided to inspect each in turn. We were the last to be inspected, so we stood stiff for about twenty minutes. It was hot, and I was amusing myself with the stone wall and the tree in my field of vision, counting the berries on the tree and so on, while feeling pretty browned off. After quarter of an hour a chap quietly folded up halfway down my rank, and was carted away. After the inspection we did a right turn and stood for a few more minutes. Some unfortunate in the next Flight slithered to the ground, and was dumped by the roadside. A minute later his neighbour followed his example. We were all sniggering quietly by this time − they were dropping off like flies. I remembered the days at school, when I used to fight during Prayers in the Hall; it was solely my mind that threatened to lay me out every time. Nowadays I have completely overcome that fear. Likewise inoculations are solely a matter of mental control. There is nothing in the actual injection, but people start thinking about it and they're out in no time.

* * * * *

A little-known YMCA in the town, and another canteen just outside, provides gramophone concerts − one on Tuesdays and the other on Thursdays. The 'Clients' are few and fairly select (all in uniform) and everyone SITS WITHOUT A SOUND and listens to the music, because that's what they came there to do. This is a revelation in a canteen, for the poor bitter music-lover (whatever they say, the taste of the Services IS lousy: it's only the few who are prepared to go out of their way for good stuff). They are going to play the *Rite of Spring* at some time in the future; I heard extracts from it when I was last on leave, and was fascinated by some of it ...

I was in the midnight to 4 a.m. shift. It was dead calm, with light cloud and a mirror-like sea, and the loveliest moonrise I have ever seen. The rim came up red and smoky, like a glare of fire, and as it rose it became golden and clear, with reflection in the slightly rippled sea. Through binoculars I watched the light on the sand, the tiny wavelets, the light writhing on the water, as if pure golden eels were flashing the whole way along the moontrack to the diffused glow on the sea horizon. Then a show started on the other side of the Channel. I could see gun-flashes reflected in the clouds and for about an hour there was an almost continuous mumble of distant explosions.

* * * * *

The relaxation of having nothing on one's mind is lovely. During the last couple of weeks before the exams I suffered from an extreme mental tension caused by overwork, which made it impossible for me to forget work and relax: in the last week it was a feeling like having a spring wound up in one's brain. Now all I do is stand around with one experienced eye fixed on the sky. It is wonderful, and I am seeing everything I have been shut away from recently. I lie on my back at the foot of the tower at midnight, watching the stars move over for hours on end.

I am off from 10 a.m. to 4 p.m. to-day, and will go to bed when I come off at 8, as I must get up at 3 to-morrow morning. I have wallowed in pure delightful aimlessness for the last three hours, since 11 a.m. I have just wandered round the town as slowly as a policeman on his beat, browsing in bookshops, wandering into Lyons for dinner, gazing at passers-by and generally letting the world go by instead of trying to race it.

* * * * *

EPISODE IN AUGUST

A humble-bee rose on the hot perfumed air of the bean-field and sailed away towards the darkness of its bordering trees. Passing through a gap in the gloomy, light-flecked cedar foliage it emerged into sunlight again in a huge garden where the heat beat down on a brown lawn below a house made sepulchral by drawn blinds. Beyond the lawn, where three human figures slowly walked, were steps leading down to a flower-garden. This was many times larger than the lawn, and laboriously planned as a labyrinth of flagged paths among bed after bed of curious, exotic blossoms wilting with thirst. In the centre glittered an ornamental pool. All the garden was harsh and still in the heat, and made sombre by the cedars which completely enclosed it.

The bee planed down towards the lawn and landed on a dry grass stem by Evelyn's elbow. It clung there in momentary exhaustion, having thighs heavy with pollen.

Evelyn lay on her belly, with her heels in the air behind her. Her head was turned to one side and pillowed on her bare arms so that she could watch the red figure that was her mother on the other side of the lawn, a vivid patch of colour in the sunlight. As she lay with her head so low, her parents and the black-dressed old woman seemed distant, remote creatures staggering through grasses up to their waists, crinkled by the heat of the surface air. Then when she lifted her head they were just a man, a woman and an old woman on a path beyond the lawn, starting to go down the terrace steps.

Her father was tall, a brilliant white figure in tennis flannels and shirt. With his wife in her scarlet dress he made a vigorous picture against the background of cedars. Between them the old woman, who was his mother, walked slowly like a tired black insect preparing to lie down and die under the merciless bronze of the sky. It was midday, and there was no cloud from horizon to horizon.

Evelyn watched them go out of sight beyond the greenhouse and immediately forgot them. A strand of her bleached hair came into her eyes, so she blew it away. It dropped back. She blew harder this time, with a little splutter which afterwards made her laugh. Her short lace frock was turned back from her thighs, which were plump and faintly golden-brown, and dead smooth. Laughing, she kicked her feet in the air. They were also plump, tiny and the colour of pale ivory. She had golden hair bleached to a whitish straw-colour, fine hair for three years old.

The sun-bright hair floated down again in front of her eyes, so she let it stay there, and looked down her nose at the trophy of the moment. It was like playing with a tiny jewel, to curl the fist around it, framing it, then to banish it with a veiling other hand. And now to bring it back again, glowing in the same place as if it had really been there all the time. The jewel was a blossom of scarlet pimpernel, which really did glow with a rich reddish-orange warmth like a tiny sun on its own, in the rough grass by the lawn's edge.

She played with it until the stem snapped and the flower disappeared in the grass. Having searched for it unsuccessfully she ceased to want it and turned over on her back, sticking her round knees up into the air and pulling her hair all across her face, so that she could not be seen.

Even the sun was puzzled, and roamed about in it, here there and everywhere, trying to find a way through. But she lay still, and was safe.

Then when she shut her eyes it was red, patterned with drifting shapes like flowers, with one bright purple one in the middle slowly fading: pale red if she closed them lightly, as she did when she was pretending to be asleep, with the lids trembling, not quite meeting, so as to watch; and deepening from scarlet through dull crimson to a purplish-blackness as she screwed them up tightly.

When she had tested these colours several times, grimacing and relaxing, she turned on her side and sat up to watch her grandfather. He had sat all morning in a wheelchair in the middle of the lawn, in an open-necked shirt with a rug on his knees, a motionless figure against the tall shadowy background of the house and trees. A brown felt hat gave no shade to his eyes, as his head was always thrown back in sleep. He seldom moved or spoke, but sat utterly serene on the lawn as long as the sun shone, which in these days was always. Every hour or so, at his own request, they turned the chair a little to keep him facing the sun. His skin was a worn brown, like an old penny, on arms and forehead, gleaming just a little with sweat; gradually his beautifully combed beard, and the mane of hair projecting from beneath the hat, were becoming less rusty-grey and more the colour of mown hay just before it is turned: a golden whiteness.

He seemed a little frightening to Evelyn, but she was fascinated by his strange beard and set brown face, and by his long arms lying as if chained along the arms of the chair, with big hands that looked strong, but drooped uselessly, like squashed starfish with their thick fingers. She respected him because he never tried to lift her off her feet, hurting under her armpits, and put his arms across her and clumsily kiss her, as other people did.

Eventually growing a little bored with his silence, she dragged herself on her belly back to the edge of the lawn, where antirrhinums made a bright tangle about the bases of tall hollyhocks. The flowers bordering the lawn were homely and seldom tended, in contrast to the almost tropical luxuriance of the lower terrace. She listened to a stifled whine inside one of the small velvety flowers which dipped and trembled until the whine became a buzz and a bee flew out, startling her. She jumped back and ruffled the grass with her clenched fist in anger, to startle the bee in turn. It rose to one of the pink hollyhock blossoms, where it gently landed and crawled inside.

Evelyn found she had uncovered a buttercup, and picked it to hold against her chin, as her mother had showed her. The delicate skin shone yellow with the light from the inside of the buttercup. Sitting back on her heels with the magical glow beneath her chin, her serious blue eyes gazing across the garden and the flaxen hair spread about her shoulders, she promised great beauty in after-life.

With the child's desire to share pleasure she carried the flower across to show her grandfather. When she stood before him her sense of equality with him faltered, but she called softly to him and held out her hand, wishing him to take the flower. He seemed soundly asleep and did not move. She waited. A pack of racing, black-winged birds came swerving across the grass and fled screaming by his head, to climb again into the sky. After they had gone his shirt-collar lifted with the air flung from their wings and fell back again.

Several minutes passed, during which Evelyn called to him and offered the flower repeatedly with no success. She lost her timidity and grew annoyed with him. Her small red mouth was trembling. A tear mounted upon one eyelid. She stamped her foot.

The stretched ancient throat gleamed in the sunlight: the fingers dangled. The eyelids, whiter than the rest of the face, remained closed in negation.

Evelyn flung the flower at him. It glanced off his left cheek and fell

James Farrar, self-portrait, aged 16.

'A' Flight 3 Squadron, Torquay, April 1942. James Farrar is fifth from right in the front row.

68

The last photo, taken in summer 1944. James is on the far right.

James and David Farrar, Bath, September 1943.

Don Powell.

Margaret Farrar, circa 1970s.

70

Coltishall 1943 – water colour of a Beaufighter by Flying Officer James Farrar, 68 Night-Fighter Squadron.

James Farrar's pencil sketch of the view from his billet (the Elfordleigh Hotel, Torquay), 1942.

James Farrar's pencil sketch of Fairwood Common, Swansea, March 1944.

James Farrar at Cambridge, 1941.

James Farrar at Bath, September 1943.

Frederick Delius, 1929.

76

Henry Williamson in the 1940s.

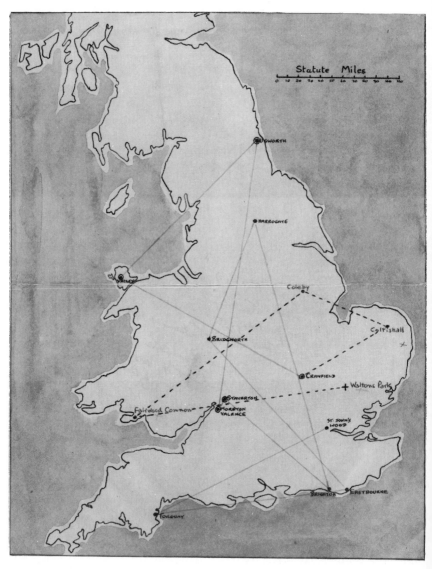

Map of the various RAF units to which James Farrar was posted; St John's Wood to Cranfield in James's own hand; completion (Cranfield to Waltons Park) by David Farrar.

78

in the shadow behind him. She ran to pick it up, kneeling terribly close so that she was frightened again, right under the shadow of his chair. In a second, between fright and anger, misery stirred in her breast. Again the buttercup was thrown at him. Then she watched in satisfaction, because although his eyes were still closed he was smiling at her a little. His mouth was slightly open, and she could just see his tongue. As he continued to smile her eyes grew large, fascinated.

There was a click in the grass beside her, but she took no notice. Something hit her foot and remained there, tickling: slowly, reluctantly taking her eyes off the old man, she looked down, wrinkling her nose in amusement to see a grasshopper preening itself on her foot.

It rubbed its shins together thoughtfully, and was gone. Somewhere in the grass nearby began a dry whirring noise like a feather being held against the spokes of a tiny revolving wheel. Evelyn looked about her, but the whirring stopped, so that she could hear other grasshoppers farther away on the lawn. Then it began again, loud and clear, nearer to her. Suddenly she saw the insect, perched by her foot on a grass stem which was exactly the colour of itself. She moved to kick it, but it flipped away first.

As she looked up again she showed her teeth and murmured rapturously at a sight of a golden bee which had alighted on her grandfather's protruding tongue. When she returned with a stick and reached up to touch it the bee was terrified and violently stung the flesh beneath it before flying away. It sailed through the still air towards the cedars, rising to pass over them and losing sight of the garden where the old man sat half-smiling.

(Winter 1942)

* * * * *

30 October 1942
We are now at the Grand Hotel, Harrogate. The first day has left the following impressions. Food not bad: disgusting amount of spit and polish – a Squadron Commander who acts as if he has little devils running around inside him. Next time we have a kit inspection we are to have the soles of our boots polished, our 'housewives' washed and ironed, and THE BACK OF OUR BOOT-BRUSHES SCRUBBED. But, cushy working hours – about four hours a day. Heard the most refreshing

pep talk of my Service career by the O.C.[1] Unit this afternoon. (We nearly always get such an address at a new station – 'You play ball with me, and I'll play ball with you,' etc.). The C.O. is tough, human, humorous, ruthless, therefore a good leader. He gave us a chance to ask questions, air grouses, and so on. It was rather hard to explain that we object to being treated as if we were I.T.W.[2] sprogs, and no one succeeded in putting this over.

About the spit and polish: we never take such things lying down. As soon as we got to the station last night they started chivvying us around. We were shocked, but we could take it. As we stood waiting I said, 'I believe they're going to turn us into airmen all over again, only we're going to break *them* in the process this time!' The bloke in front said in a reassuring voice, 'Yes, they'll soon get into our ways!' It turned out afterwards that they had no idea who we were, and fancied we were a lot of new recruits just up from St. John's Wood.

We had an all-day journey down here. We changed at Birmingham, where we had two hours' wait, just nice for lunch, we thought. But there was no transport from one station to the other, so we had to cart both our kitbags through the crowded streets, with great-coats and all webbing on, and I had packed my kitbag so efficiently that its weight nearly killed me. After this we had only twenty minutes in which to feed ourselves, in Business-Man's Birmingham in the middle of the lunch hour. Two of us dashed into the first place we saw, a real Grill Room Restaurant *à la* £5,000-a-year stockbroker. And there, surrounded by just such people, we wangled a special quick service and got a meal down with a couple of drinks, all in twenty minutes. It cost 4s. 1d. each, including tip. Phew!

We changed again at York. On the journey there we organized a jolly good system of rushing-out-of-the-train-to-the-refreshment-rooms-and-getting-some-buns-and-tea-and-rushing-back-into-the-train-before-it-left-the-station. We did this at nearly every big station where we stopped, with varying success. We had all pinched a mug from the dear old RAF at Bridgnorth, so there was no trouble over that. At Derby it was wonderful. We lined up in the corridor, mug in hand, and the moment the train stopped we were all out and running like mad to the

---

[1] Officer Commanding.
[2] Initial Training Wing.

YMCA we had spotted. The place was empty, they were all ready for us, grabbing our mugs and filling them with great efficiency, showing they must have been used to such things. In no time we were back on the train with gallons of tea and piles of lovely buns!

We had about an hour and a half to spare at York. Here things were better organized, so we were able to get tea and see a bit of the town, which made a nice break. It was great fun being dumped in a strange town for an hour or two and enjoying someone else's town, after so much of having to make a town as much one's own as possible. York looked rather a nice place, though rather too City-ish. The river looks just like the Thames.

* * * * *

5 November 1942
Heard from Don to-day. He seems much more on top of the world, in fact pretty cocky. He had leave a fortnight ago, and had a good time with Jean (who writes to him, he says, three times a week).

I enquired about Aubrey in my last letter to him, though I felt it might not be wise – so many young acquaintances have 'had it' lately. He has been a prisoner of war in Germany for about six weeks. The elder Jolly (at school with me) has had it as a Sergeant Pilot. Also George Couch. Also D. H. Harris, who was in Classical 5 with me. And I just feel a bloody waster.

They have given *everything* that ever man was privileged to have, and to what end? So that we should scrounge around month after month, and chuckle over our scrounges, sneaking round the corner for a smoke, hiding from official eyes in some back street. Our problem being not how to use every moment fully, how to get into the war as quickly and efficiently as possible, how to surmount the dangers which would try to kill us; but how best to *fill in* a morning, which place is the safest to hide away, how to keep ourselves amused.

That is the secret of my new sense of frustrated browned-offness. It's not like the little old grouse 'we want to be posted.' It's a big unreasonable thing which embraces the whole war, the wearing frustration of filling in a morning while others are being killed for lack of support. Of course, it doesn't affect me at the time in such a concrete manner, but it has been present as an undertone, and this is the first time I have nailed it down to words. On reading this again I can see that the hammer has missed more than it has hit, but I am just scribbling this down without any pre-consideration or revision, and that explains its lack of lucidity.

I want to get into the war; but my last reason would be the popular one of dying for a cause. I am not interested in avoiding death, but this again is not through any willingness to 'lay down my life for my country.' It's just that I can't tolerate fake existence, most of all when it is permitted to continue through the sacrifices of people no different from myself who are living and dying *really*.

So under my superficial, normal ups and downs of life I am very much down. God knows what will ever happen to put this right, the way things are shaping now. I came in after a chance to do a job which was not divorced from reality and necessity; and instead I am playing in an ironic puppet show away behind the scenes, not in the war at all, but in a bureaucratic cloud-cuckoo land.

* * * * *

Brighton, Winter 1942

For the past few evenings I have been writing a story in the YMCA until about 9 p.m., then over to my favourite canteen for supper, and back in the Met at 9.30 or 9.45, having read the manuscript over at supper. I was thoroughly ashamed of myself on New Year's Eve because that is how I spent my evening, while everyone else in Brighton was getting canned. (Sighs of relief from Mother.) All the boys came in pickled, and there was I standing about with an ill-fitting halo in a sort of whited-sepulchre attitude. Very degrading. People were coming in yelling all night and throwing dustbin lids down the stairs (ninety-seven steps) which made quite a noise.

But I was awfully happy next morning when all the poor devils had hangovers except me. So the moral is, DRINK *GOOD* BEER.

Where I sat finishing the job at a typewriter, people came popping in all the evening to ask if there were any beds going, and could they use the 'phone, and was there a place to wash, and somebody said could they borrow the ink: which was not conducive to good work, but I managed somehow. The story is rather long, several thousand words (haven't counted them yet).

82

JOHNNY BEYOND

Several seats banged somewhere away to my right, and people began to move out sideways, towards me. I had seen just about enough, so bidding farewell to an amorous Crosby I gathered up my coat and left before the knee-pushers reached me. We drifted like iron filings to the illuminated magnet EXIT.

As always, this seemed to be a different exit from any I had encountered before in the Metropole, having labyrinthine corridors, thick-carpeted, whose umbered walls echoed soft conversation and laughter. Less sumptuous stone steps, a clanging iron door, and then I was in a dark side street. Quickening my pace I came to Victoria Street, crossed almost under the bonnet of a quietly lumbering 'bus, and called in at the Milk Bar for a sausage roll and a cup of tea. A soft-lit haven full of women's chatter and the strange provincial voices of soldiers on their way through London.

Then I walked along to the Tube. Under a faintly starry sky 'buses soughed past, there was a leisurely mingling of small and large feet walking in step, low voices of girls. The pavements of Victoria are after-dark promenades for army boots and high-heeled shoes; the barred shop doorways harbour many silent undiscovered couples.

This is how I like it. Footsteps and voices, intimacy unseen at one's elbow. This is the London in which I, child of nature, professing scorn of towns, can bring myself to be happy. An opened door swings a beam of light on to a pair in front of me, a WAAF ACW[1] on the arm of a sergeant, a flying man I believe. She is speaking, her voice has a husky cadence which makes me happy.

A hot gust of ozone announced the Tube station, dim blue-lit like a cavern. I got my thin wartime ticket and went down to the platform whistling, at peace with the world. Trains at this time were not frequent, so for nearly ten minutes I leaned against the enamel announcement VICTORIA and studied the uniforms of half the allied nationalities. A Polish Army officer, casual, but ill at ease, with that curious angular cap; New Zealand airmen, a little drunk – sibilant accents blurred; three Canadian gunners trying to get off with a garrulous trio of East London girls, who were ignoring the men, but at the same time anxious

---

[1] Aircraft Woman.

not to lose them. Two French privates, tankmen, segregated by language, a flaxen-haired Nordic, some sailors bearing a long Dutch-looking word on their caps. Poor chaps, I thought, all at sixes and sevens with the English language and therefore, presumably, with the English girls. Although I did notice two Polish pilot-officers conveying a great deal to a WAAF by means of sign-language of very little ambiguity.

The air began to move, women porters yelled, packs were lifted, steel helmets clashed and heavy boots clumped after me as I made for an unlit coach because it rang with singing voices. It was the older type of coach, and I found my way to one of the double seats, whose opposite number was occupied by two dark shapes. The singing stopped. Quiet for a moment, then the train jerked into motion.

The lights came on. Everyone looked around at everyone else and then proceeded to look at nothing with that evident interest which only an Englishman in a railway carriage can simulate. That is, all except the ATS[1] girls at the far end, and the various soldiers who seemed to be attached to them in a vague sort of way.

I was one of three in mufti. All the rest, nearly capacity, were in uniform. Facing me sat a fine pair, an observer in the Royal Air Force and a dark girl of ideal beauty. Beyond them, a WAAF junior officer, very sedate and cultured, talking to a Wing Commander: they faced three men of the Royal Artillery who leaned forward, cigarettes fuming in leathery hands, and peered at the Inner Circle map pasted opposite. A sergeant air-gunner of not more than nineteen lounged in the doorway.

It was pleasant for me just to wedge myself in the corner of my seat and watch. I loved to assess − or try to assess − people's characters; it was my substitute for the crossword puzzles many folk do in trains. The young WAAF officer was simple. She had been to a respectable high school, where she learned of those mighty institutions, Fair Play and Strict Morality; converses well, no aberrations for her: she sleeps chastely in her own bed. Oh, yes, I am young and have got everything taped.

When I had settled her my gaze returned many times to the observer opposite, and more particularly to his companion, the quietly voluble beauty. He a New Zealander, brown-eyed, full-lipped, somewhat elfin in a stolid sort of way: but she, aged about twenty, too pale like all

---

[1] Auxiliary Territorial Service.

Londoners, dark hair curven behind ears and dispread on shoulders: smart in a light fawn coat, a delicious poise to her body, young-breasted, with perfect limbs: child-faced. She, unthinking, the incarnation of serenity which is utterly beyond me.

They seemed to be very intimate. I could not understand her eyes, which had that deep enigmatic purity only to be found in the eyes of young women, which I like to think is the shadowed agelessness of a naked Eve. But I could see he loved her, and from the gentle urgency of her voice and the way she toyed with his hand I decided it was mutual. He was sitting back with his brown eyes resting somewhere beyond my left shoulder. From time to time she pinched his hand playfully. I understood his absent air. He was perhaps off to operational flying again, and was rapt with a feeling of dissolution. I also knew his leave to be ending because the girl was not questioning him, only speaking of petty things. When they first meet he must recount everything he has seen and done: but on the way back the conversation is desperately everyday, a mind-barrier of words.

Why *was* he so sullen with his eyes beyond me? Suddenly I felt he was not in a reverie after all, but all looking at something. So I turned casually, and SAW.

The man with his back to the window, behind me, wore the uniform of a Pilot-Officer, an air-gunner. I looked at his head, then down at his feet and, transfixed, raised my eyes slowly. HE HAD NO FACE.

As I live, no visible features. It was not just a wound, that dull gash which makes a mockery of an eye or the expression of a mouth. No, the memory of this went deep into my consciousness. Half his head was bandaged still, but the other half, towards me, was just a dirty smear. Do you remember that soggy windfall apple you picked up last autumn after the wasps had left it, a half sphere? That is how his face looked.

I turned to the window, in whose darkness the tunnel cables oscillated frenziedly. We were travelling at speed. Then I became aware of the faint image of the nodding mushroom of bandages, wraith-like, against the outer darkness. The roar broke and the poster-chequered brilliance of Charing Cross went streaming past, banishing the image. For a moment, as we stopped, the lights went out, and magically my mind became active:

When I entered the train the lights were out. They had been out for some time, because when they came on, soldiers with full kit began to study the Underground map as if it were new to them, besides all those who had got on the train with me.

Once more I turned, this time in trepidation, to observe the three inexperienced-looking Canadians opposite this man. They regarded the map above him, or the youngster in the doorway, or me, or the couple facing me. But there was one place where they would not look, and that was at the man straight in front of them.

'Behind you is a faceless man, the man beyond the war whom we all forget. In front are a man and a woman in love, who came into this coach in darkness, not seeing what was beyond your seat. The lights came on for the first time after you had sat down. Now you are faced with a carefree, happy girl and a man whose life can go out at any moment like a candle-flame: her lover who can see what she cannot, because your seventy-three-and-a-half inches oppose only her sight. The 'if' of which she is unaware, the incarnation of failure the sight of which would stop her talking like a tap turned off. He can see, and is afraid for her easy optimism, lest you move.'

I set my shoulders back to broaden them, held in fascination by the thought of the single wing these two men wore, and the pitiable simplicity of reducing one to the state of the other. Thinking, too, of my undismayed aspiration to a wing almost identical. Wondering if one day I shall sit in an Underground train with people who are afraid to look at me.

'The climax is not for your eyes, because you yourself are the climax. If you like, when we stop at the Monument, turn from the door and see what you have done, the space you have left, the dull stare in her eyes, the silent mouth.'

We pulled out of Mansion House. The tunnel closed in again, and the ATS girls started a new song, to the tune of *Mademoiselle from Armentières*. It was something about the WRNS and the WAAFS, who they declared vehemently, did *not* win the war. It was, of course, the ATS. I pulled out my notebook and began to copy it down. The final verse was the trumpet blast to bring down the walls of Babylon. The army, in our coach, took on a new expression, shifting uncomfortably in its seats. Cat-calls began to fly around.

I turned over a page of my notebook and three paragraphs came up and hit me. The date was a week before:

'I saw a young man in Leadenhall Market to-day who travelled by means of two sticks, between which his legs dangled stiffly. He wore an old blue suit.

'It was a shock to see the R.A.F.V.R. badge on his lapel, common symbol of deferred service, the badge which I wear. The difference being that I was on the way in and he on the way out.

'What happens to these husks who went in like all of us, energetic and enthusiastic, and who emerge broken, useless, the war over for them?'

There was Cannon Street spinning away into darkness, anyhow, and I was due to get out at the next station. Can you imagine what it is to sit as stiff as a poker merely because of someone's eyes which are not even looking at you? To be forbidden to take handkerchief from your pocket because it involves leaning sideways ever so slightly, which simple act explodes a world for two people? I was staking everything on the chance that they too might get off at the Monument, in which case I would safeguard their ephemeral world from detonation for the last few minutes. You see, the spirit of farewell is so important, because it remains with one until the next meeting. And how could I let them depart with the image of that broken man before them?

Then it happened. There was a movement behind me, and I looked round to see him turbaned and ghastly, going stiffly to the door. With that disfigurement the fact that he was blind seemed a mere detail. But he couldn't get out, we were in the tunnel at speed! Hopelessly I looked at the other air-gunner, the boy, who continued to lounge against an upright as if nothing would ever startle him. Somehow I couldn't move myself. 'In Heaven's name, don't!' I yelled, but he pulled open the door and walked clean out in a searing flash of light. He just vanished into the tunnel without a sound. But nobody stirred. They had not even looked at him. He might never have been there at all, for all they showed.

Frantically I appealed to the couple opposite, didn't you see what happened? They stared at me as if I was mad. The girl's lovely eyes were upon me in faint scorn, for about a minute, then they suddenly dilated, and with a gesture of disgust she buried her face in her hands. Then raising her face again, flaming-eyed, she sobbed hysterically at me, 'Oh, how can I look at you any more, you've got no face, NO FACE!' The eyes burning me up, a pulsing blackness thumping me like heavy wings, I screamed in utter agony, the eyes before me, incandescent, losing purity, hard and bitter, a man's eyes – larger

87

and larger — then shrinking, shrinking to a stony vagueness, wings, white wings, Oh, God, am I a bloody angel, white wings, white arms out in the breakers tirelessly tossing, tirelessly tossing, tirelessly tossing, that's Whitman, what the hell's Whitman to do with it. White wings shrinking, no angel, there's RAF in the middle of them, that's not angelic. Waves ebbing, I'm stranded with a singing in my ears in a white peace. There's Phil bending over me. I wish he'd take those cursed wings off. A small clean hospital room, flowers and a gorgeous nurse moving round. Now she has gone and the door is closed. Smell of death disguised in antiseptics. 'Hullo, Phil, how's life? I am told that when I came round I was yelling, "CHRIST, what's this, have I jumped off the train?"'

'Hullo, sonny, what's all this train talk? Going back to childhood days again?'

'What am I doing here, I ought not to be in bed, am I hurt?'

'Sonny boy,' said Phil — he always talked like that (he is dead now) — 'you are recovering from your first write-off in the arms of a beeyootiful nurse. I always said you night-fighter blokes had the cushiest job. By the way, Alice is coming in in a minute — you remember that smashing brunette we met at the dance? You know the girl in the light fawn coat. I think someone stands a chance there.'

'Phil, I can't possibly let her see me,' I pleaded anxiously. Every time I spoke something hammered in my head. He told me I talked as if I had twelve hangovers rolled into one.

'And why not, O bashful one?'

'MY FACE, Phil. Is it too awful?'

'No, old boy, I am afraid the ugly old pan has not changed one whit. Although you *did* come a cropper.'

'Oh, Lord, yes,' I laughed weakly. 'Johnny and I did bend something last night, didn't we?'

'Yes, you were quite unkind to your pretty Beau. Only it was *five* days ago. No, to tell the truth I wonder that you ever came out of that crate alive. Two of the boys are making ashtrays out of it — they were the only chaps who could find bits big enough for ashtrays.'

'Lying swine. By the way, how's Johnny? Have they been practising fretwork on his innards too?'

'Sorry, chum. There is no Johnny.'

'Oh.'

He sat down by the bed. The room was bright and quiet, but outside there were some kids shouting.

'Phil.'

'Yes?'

'I have just seen myself at seventeen. It was damned funny. You know, dramatic, egotistical, highflown words and all that. Couldn't light a fag without nearly choking myself. I'd clean forgotten what it was like. And one's conception of things − melodramatic isn't the word!'

'Five days to dream of pretty women, eh? I think I'll go out and get myself cracked up.' (He never dreamed, when he did.)

'No,' I said, 'it's not all fun. Tell me what happened to Johnny and me. Did we come down a wallop? I think we got one first.'

'Well, cobber, it was like this. You wiped up one all right, an 88 loaded right up to the dicky. He came down like a slow meteor, scattering fireworks on all sides. Lit the whole place up when he hit the deck. Carried out all his own funeral ceremony, burial and all. All we've got to do is put the crosses up.

'Then Johnny seemed to go nuts. Honestly, I've never seen anything like it. In less time than it takes to tip a wink to a dame, you'd come down from about eighteen grand − pardon my American − to more or less floor level. Think of a Beau in a power-dive. She pulled out somehow − but the speed that fool tried to set her down! Believe me, you came in over the flare-path at something over three hundred. Cumulative effect of dive. Well, no landing ground was made to hold that, so she just beetled flat out through a shed and went skating. Sat down at a far end of Mucky Field in some poor unfortunate's drawing-room. They found you on the settee or something, you low hound, which is probably why you are here now. In the name of Heaven, what bit him?'

'I think we ran into some of our own flak,' I told him. 'Our chaps can't hit a Hun for love or money, but when it comes to Beaus − well − that's different.'

We were silent for a moment. Then:

'It's funny you should have asked about disfigurement,' said Phil slowly. 'You see, I don't much like telling you, but poor old Johnny caught it badly. He went forward into his instrument panel and it took his face clean off.'

* * * * *

We arrived at Staverton Camp, Gloucester, on the Saturday night, January 9 1943. First impressions were of mud, darkness, mud, inability to find one's way about, mud, bitter cold, mud. We are in a hut, luckily not a Nissen. It takes a bit of getting used to after hotels, but we will manage. The mess and NAAFI are quite near. The former is smallish, no-queueing, cheerful service, good food and *a wireless on all the time*! Such touches as this show that we are in a different Air Force. In 54 Group a wireless in the mess would be 'prejudicial to good discipline' or some such rubbish. So feeding is a pleasure. And we enjoy our meals for a change, because there are now no visits to tea-shops all day to ruin the appetite. The joy of the mess and NAAFI is the lack of crowds.

Ablutions less pleasant. This morning, when I went to wash before breakfast, the place began to be revealed. Gleam of bog-water all around. In misty half-light, several large aircraft squatted cowled and tarpaulined not far from our hut. I could only just see their outlines, but it meant a lot.

When it got light the visibility was poor and there was nothing but mud and mist, various odd buildings and the aircraft. We chased all over the place filling in forms and seeing various departments, and all the other attendant nuisances of arrival. We got to know the place a bit. It *is* a real aerodrome. We saw two of the Ansons in which we are to fly. In fact we were due to fly this afternoon, but weather remained duff so it was scrubbed. Naturally the first flight will be a terrific event.

* * * * *

It was. We felt an awful lot of nobs waddling round to the parachute dept. in 'outers' and flying boot, complete with maps. We drew our 'chutes, signed for them, then went out by the hangars to wait for the crew lorry. This took us round the perimeter to the Ansons. They carry three cadets, pilot and W/Op. We did a lot of taxying around the place before the pilot finally opened her up and took off.

There is too much to describe fully, especially in the first trip when everything is so strange. We went down across the Severn first and then did a round trip over several towns and back to base. We did an hour and fifty minutes.

The Anson is no luxury kite and there is a hell of a lot of noise and vibration. Williams was airsick after a time, but Watson and I were

O.K. I wouldn't say I felt completely normal; it was the turns that seemed to tie knots in one's innards. It is queer to see a place revolving past your tilted wing-tip, and gravity, centrifugal force and other weird things make you wonder exactly where your stomach is going to end up. Flying was luckily pretty smooth. Later on the pilot did a couple of deliberate stalls just to amuse us. Poor old Williams was sitting in the back having lost all interest in the proceedings. I was at that time in front beside the pilot. Our nose went up and up, you could see the wing-tips canted up at a steep angle; the warning hooter screamed that 'you mustn't throttle back when your undercarriage is retracted' (a safety device). She just hung on the air, then suddenly the whole nose (and us) went *right* down with a sickening lurch; everything seemed to fall away from around us. It was remarkable how quickly she picked up out of it.

We had to map-read (or rather try to map-read) the whole way. I did quite well on parts, average on others, and on one leg was completely lost. However, even the pilot wasn't sure of himself on that leg, as he afterwards admitted.

Eventually we were back over the 'drome and came in to a very nice landing. I got out feeling rather deaf (change of air pressure) and not quite ready for tea (but pretty good under the circumstances) and in a few minutes the deafness had worn off and I went and ate a good tea with immense gusto. I really felt good.

Second time up I was more at home, less excited and therefore more settled. And I thoroughly enjoyed it. After the first time my stomach never thought twice about turning itself around. Even on the turns it kept facing the same way, and there were no effects at all. Whereas on the first fight I saw things tilting and said, 'Whoops, here we go,' on the second I merely circled the place and said, 'Lovely.' I was surprised at how different it felt.

We couldn't find our kite with the rest and had to walk halfway across the 'drome before we located it. There were no erks about and the pilot and W/Op. got in and started moaning like anything about it. It was one of those flying coffins. When we were in the briefing room an officer had come in and said, 'Sergeant Crump, have you flown a flapless aircraft before?' and everyone seemed to turn round and say good bye to us.

Still, it got off the ground and flew. The windows were so filthy you could hardly see anything. Map-reading was difficult. When I went up the front the view was better. At one point I was following every lane and ditch almost on a quarter-inch map. It came along just as it should have done. I was bucked. We flew at about two thousand feet. Railways and water are superb recognition points – water gleams bright and trails of steam often betray a railway. Woods, roads and so on, are other things I looked for. I felt more at home with things this afternoon, and physically I felt grand the whole time. It was a bit cold, however.

*   *   *   *   *

17 January 1943
The work at present is quite hard enough to leave one pretty tired by the end of the day, after our six months of inaction, but it is not as hard as it will be. I am happy here in spite of the weather and the mud: it's grand to have a real job to do, and now the job has reached such a practical stage it demands all one's energy and most of one's time. To-day is the first time I have been able to feel expansive since I arrived here, the first feeling of relaxation. The nose-to-the-grindstone effect prevents me seeing or thinking very far from my environment. As an illustration, I was genuinely surprised the other day when for no reason at all I realized that spring would eventually come to this wintry place. You tend to accept the mud and cold as permanent surroundings, and you are seldom detached enough from factual thinking to remember seasons, ideas, and other broad and only semi-tangible influences. This putting-aside of aesthetic life is going to have its advantages because it will make the day-off and especially the ultimate leave (touch wood!) much greater occasions than they would otherwise have been. On my recent leaves I was merely transferring a lazy life from Eastbourne or Brighton to Carshalton: there was no real holiday-feeling about it, because how can you have holidays when you are unemployed?

I observed a renowned and beautiful aerial effect the other afternoon. It is called Halo. We were about twenty miles from base, over a strange town on a hillside called Great Malvern, which is remarkable to its location, the inhabitants being like cliff-cave-dwellers only they live in houses. We flew past some cumulus cloud at about four thousand feet (billowing cauliflower cloud). It looked like genuine cotton-wool in the sunlight, really lovely. Then I noticed a spectrum-coloured halo flitting over it, enclosing the tiny shadow of the aircraft. I forget how it is caused, some atmospheric effect, but I have read about it and was very bucked actually to see it. It looks so strange you can't believe it at first. The halo is mostly coppery with blue diffusions, but also has tinges of other colours.

* * * * *

Returning from Clevedon, am filled with contentment: happy with memories of a beautiful sunny day, early mist over the wooded hills and valleys seen from Walton Castle, the sea-like expanse of Severn Estuary with lovely skies over the Welsh hills; of Delius' music – *Over the Hills and Far Away, Fennimore and Gerda, Sea-Drift,* casting the old spell of beauty and serenity. Of a fresh spring-like evening with a dusk-blue sky streaked with cirrus, and in the west tinges of spectrum-colour on the Welsh cumulus. Later a red smoky sunset out of which the Bristol train approached down gleaming blood-red rails.

I like to remember the crumbling, bird-haunted ruin of Walton Castle where it stood sentinel over misty distances of valley and wooded hill. The sky at that time was grey all over, but brimming with light where the sun lay concealed. A little light rain fell. Golfers moved over the slopes, we could hear their voices at a distance. Everything was damp, and still.

And the records,[1] words cannot do justice to them. Delius it is and shall be for ever more. My temperament seems so suited to his idiom that to listen to his music is like hearing myself speak with some borrowed eloquence, self-expression in another's terms; yet how suited those terms are to what I have to say.

The morning, the evening, the music were in one mood, which brought peace into my mind ...

* * * * *

The other afternoon we flew over 10/10 cloud for the first time. I felt very cut off from the world: the cloud seemed to form an extensive and mountainous world of its own, a blank cotton-wool layer to which there was no end, and out of which arose queer bumps and heaps. A darker layer in the distance was like a mountain range, and it was difficult to believe that it wasn't. The sky above varied in colour from violet to eggshell-blue. But when I was trying like hell to find a gap

---

[1] Evidently the second Delius Society album (Beecham and the London Philharmonic) issued in 1938, reissued in LP format in 1976).

through which I could endeavour to find where I was, so as to please my Flight Commander, it was no holiday-time.

* * * * *

I heard a fox barking early this morning beyond the eastern boundary of the aerodrome. It was just beginning to get light, but the moon was still the only noticeable radiance. The 'drome was a misty pool of silence beyond which the distant Cotswolds lay etched in uneven line. The sky was dark silky-blue, moonlight and starlight gleamed in the water about the hut. Aptly in this pre-dawn stillness came the husky double bark, mysterious compared with the happy shout of the dog: answered by another several fields away.

* * * * *

I had quite a nice lie-in this morning until 8 o'clock of which the last hour (when I was awake) was a warm and comfortable reverie which made me feel life was worth while. Then just before 9 o'clock, in came the local Flight-Sergeant (a living example of Air Force authorization of people of fifth-rate intelligence to treat others like dirt) and nattered about 'why weren't those beds made up' and 'the fireplace was dirty' and the one remaining chap in bed had no right to be there just because it was his day off. That is how much of a holiday is allowed to you on your one day off per week. This didn't worry me because I had my bed made up and floor-space swept, but I resent the attitude. What civilian has not the right to *have* some rest on his day of rest?

* * * * *

There is a story of one of our Canadian sergeant W/Op. A.G.s who went into a shop in Cheltenham to buy a protractor. No, he couldn't have one, they could only be sold to WAR WORKERS.

* * * * *

When I go out in the morning, I cycle along the path between meadow and ploughed-field, and past a wood out on to the main road. The stars are brilliant and it is still nearly dark. There are three tall elms and a shorter one in a group opposite our hut, across the meadow, which frame Orion every morning. Sirius glitters brightest at this time, because the air is frosty. Only occasionally are the fields and fences rimed.

94

Usually it is a soft darkness with trees silhouetted against the gleam breaking over the Cotswolds, and the stars burn like lamps above. On my way to the road I pass cattle in the meadow, dim shapes recumbent as they have been all night.

After work, we go straight to tea as it is on the way from 'drome to hut, and leave the 'Communal Site' to return like labourers to the home, and the labourer's contentment after work possesses me. I think this is perhaps the happiest part of the day, and I whistle like any ploughboy hopping home over the clods. And some people (not many) are cheesed here!

It isn't all due to the surroundings. There is a sense of the work being the main thing and buttons, etc. (for the first time) not of prior importance. Two people since I came here have said, 'You'll find this a happy station,' and they are just about right. Everyone cycles about doing his job, the aircraft go into the air, the cadets navigate them, the orderly room people work in the orderly room, flight-sergeants give orders instead of being moronic prodnoses, and generally the place *runs*. Flying is taken seriously, you get a long and extensive briefing, in fact no less thorough than an Ops. briefing. I have got to be First Navvy to-morrow morning (I am still waiting my turn) so I hope I can cope.

* * * * *

Ten seconds from the hut door takes me into the country. The way is over a green and rotten fence reinforcing the hedge, then I follow along the hedge, by which runs a ditch, to a place where the stream itself comes across the meadow to meet me, and hurries busily away to my left, curving again to the right round the cluster of trees. I cross it by a decayed wooden bridge, and bear left to follow the stream. The first thing that strikes me about it is the depth, speed and dirty colour of it: much of the land here lies under water, and every watercourse is brimful and muddy-coloured, completely opaque. Over this part of the stream hang thick clumps of brambles, through which in places I have to peer to see the turgid water. Farther on the stream-bed splits, one fork turns right, widens and becomes the respectable, classic water-setting towards the house: the other goes on, surges down a miniature weir of rocks and bends round to the right.

Inside the bend, among the trees, is an ancient summerhouse. What gaiety it must have seen in summers of the past! − as I sit down in it I am looking straight up the sheet of water at the house, like the popular picture of the Taj Mahal. A typical retreat of Victorian gentry. But now the thatch is soft and rotted, bored by rats, and mossy inside. Straw and thatch-rubbish lie on the grey earthy floor, disused birds' nest inside the eaves. The place is derelict, and the seasons are slowly breaking it down.

On the ground inside lies a dead otter. This is the first I have ever seen, but how could I help knowing every detail of it after reading *Tarka*?[1] The pelt is loose in places, flapping apart from the jaws which snarl so impressively when I pull them open; head and belly are a dirty grey mess of maggots, and the summerhouse is stale with putrefaction. How the otter died I do not know. But its presence points to one thing: this water is a hunting-ground of the otters, so if I look and listen well, I may find them. At any rate, I may hear their cries one night along the river-bank.

Leaving the rotting shelter I pick my way among the trees to the banks of the mere — my name for the stretch of water. At midday the sun shines across this, and on the exposed southern banks I hope very soon to find primroses. Already among the trees, in suitable ground, the primrose-leaves are large, so large that they should very soon frame the flowers. And spring cannot be mistaken here: there are the spotted leaves of the arum-lily, fragile fern-leaves of wood anemone, shoots of the ever-prolific elder, and some strange plants actually in flower, thick stems without leaves, but crowned with tiny mauve flowers which have the scent of heliotrope. Hazel saplings round about are hung with long pale catkins: and the sunlight itself, seen from among cedars and beeches, illumining huge white cumulus clouds, is springlike as it falls on the boggy ground.

At the banks of the mere are the stems of last year's reeds, and flax bearing straggly beards, leaning this way and that, swaying in the wind. There is a language about this water's-edge in winter; a risping of death on death on death, a mere whisper of decay stirred by the wind, as the brown sere flag-leaves dip to the water and touch one another. A moorhen scuttles away as I approach, but otherwise there might be no life about this water at all. The colour of it is the same, thick and greyish, and the reflections of trees opposite are olive-green across its surface.

---

[1] *Tarka the Otter*, by Henry Williamson.

The whisper of death goes on along its banks, but soon I notice that the water *lives*. The surface is broken all over with tiny tremblings, not even ripples, which represent the slight current. It shimmers, pale grey.

I can hear the rushing of the waterfall where the stream splits, reminding me of the millpool at the bottom of the Manaccan Lawnfield, where I used to watch the shadows of ripples slide like golden straws over the clear stony stream-bed. How unlike this dull expanse of water with its ruined sedges among the winter trees, where only a little pale sunlight and the crinkled leaves of primroses and elder-shoot promise the coming summer. ...

The above writing is lousy stuff because it is solely factual, entirely unembellished by any sort of imagination, but the subject-matter is there and I just can't get on to an imaginative basis when I am acting as U/T Navigator again − the two very different types of brain required just won't live together in the same head.

*   *   *   *   *

Strange heraldic symbolism in Gloucester Cathedral tombs. The deceased and wife repose in stone on the coffin lid, some of them ancient warriors, the wives dutiful and meek even in representation of death. At the feet of the man is usually some creature: a dog in the case of a fighting man, often a falcon of a generalized type for a man of justice, and the one King (who died in A.D. 729) is favoured with a lion.

Talked to two dear old buffers in Lyons' tea-shop about youth, inexperience, and so on. Oh, sorrowful land of Never-Again, the spirit without the flesh!

*   *   *   *   *

Ten Ansons are ranged along the perimeter track, warming up as we arrive. How nice it would be to see a *different* aircraft for a change: but there they are, Anson after Anson, all shaking and muttering to themselves, dull with the same dirt, streaked from engine cowling to trailing-edge with the same oil, some with dented nacelles, some with bleary windows, some sunk in mire. The most amazing thing in the face of this ugly-duckling appearance is their undoubted reliability. Touch wood.

The eleventh aircraft, which is ours, is silent. Nevertheless, we get in and distribute ourselves around. The pilot looks bored, and I sit beside him looking down at the ruffled head of an erk between engine and fuselage. The rest of the erk is winding desperately at a very unco-operative engine. The propeller moves round as he winds, slowly and without enthusiasm, as propellers always do before they make that very unexpected lunge and decapitate the unwary. Once or twice it flickers and stops again. The erk pauses to release a very commonplace word on the wind, and I like to think that strengthens the petrol, for next time the engine condescends to start. We vibrate gently while the erk fastens down the flap in the nacelle and disappears under the nose, after which the other propeller flickers, whirls and all but disappears and we are enclosed in a small hell of noise from which the aircraft is apparently trying to free itself by shaking. Now there is nothing to do for several minutes, but sit and watch the oiltemperature rising, while the kite trembles and shivers and bumps about against the chocks. At this stage the navigator must trap all his instruments in large hands on his tilted table, or the Duty Gremlin will confiscate them. The vibration is terrific. At last the pilot is satisfied and signs for the aircraft's efficiency. The door is slammed and we are ready to move off.

Chocks away, we are engulfed in an almighty sound as the engines strive to pull their attendant wheels out of the mud. With a sudden lurch we are free and the pilot quickly throttles back. Then we turn and taxy to the runway. Taxying is all motive force and cancellation, the throttles go forward and back as is required, brakes go on and off with a gasp of compressed air. You turn a little to the left and the left throttle lever must go forward; this proves too much, you swing to the right, brake, and rev-up right again. Sometimes you get a clear run of twenty or thirty yards, bouncing along smoothly like a well-sprung 'bus.

We queue up for the use of the runway while three aircraft in turn move to the end, pause, turn, pause again, and with a perceptible fading of the propeller-whirl begin to move forward, tail lifting, gathering speed and lifting, touching, lifting again and starting to climb.

Now it is our turn. We pivot on one stationary wheel and face the wind with the whole broad, sooty expanse of the runway before us. For a moment we, too, pause. Then both throttle levers go right forward, hard up against the panel, and on full boost we begin to move, slowly at first, but gradually more freely, the grass speeding up till it rushes past on either side. It is an exhilarating moment, you are hurling yourself at the far end of the 'drome with all you've got, and for a long time the kite refuses to lift. Bump, bump, lighter, suddenly dead smooth, down to bump again, a last bump almost a caress of the ground and it is smoothness again and we surge up over the boundary trees with blank sky beyond the nose.

*   *   *   *   *

Twenty minutes before Base we commence a glide on course from ten thousand feet. Up here it is quite hot in the sunlight, but we can see that near the ground it will be dull. Broken cotton-wool layers of stratocumulus lie like waste lands as far as we can see. They are at two thousand feet, and don't worry us for a long time.

With airspeed at 85 m.p.h. the surging roar has ceased: slightly nose-down, the kite rests on the air gently sinking, with a singing noise, and everyone has a sense of relaxation. No vibration, the engine muted and the props just meandering round. It is quite strange to *see* the whirl of your propellers.

Minute after minute we go on. Nobody says a word. We just watch the distant world which imperceptibly we are approaching. On XX[1] hill there are two clouds anchored like little white Zeppelins in a patch of clear sky. Far beyond there is a glimmer of the river-bends. Slowly we sink towards the cloud layer.

For a moment as we approach it the pilot opens up the engines and we cloud-hop, skimming the main layer and cutting through the shaggy upflung wisps and peaks which stand before us, slowly growing, and suddenly fling themselves about us. This is one of the few occasions in the air when you get a genuine impression of the speed at which you are going, as the host of spectral peaks raise their arms towards you and suddenly dash past like ferocious ghosts.

The engines die, vision blurs and for a moment we fly blinded through greyness which shuts in the engine-noise on us. We break cloud without warning at a modest two thousand feet, quite near to Base. The 'drome is an unbelievably small patch of green scarred by three black ribbons, among even smaller fields. We've got to land on one of those ribbons.

When we begin to circle the place it seems, happily, a little larger. But the second navigator cannot look any more because he has to wind

---

[1] Probably Bredon Hill.

down the undercarriage, one hundred and fifty turns approximately. All the time we are losing height, sometimes banking suddenly to keep near the 'drome. When the undercarriage handle sticks and the green indicator knobs protrude from their sheaths in front of me, we throttle right back and begin to glide in from a distance of about a mile. The pilot glances anxiously around, judging height, drift, distance; everything is in his hands now. While we put away maps and collect up our gear, and the wireless operator reels in his aerial, the pilot is like a being from another world, heavy with responsibility. Still watching ahead, he leans sideways and pumps away at his flap lever, 'squeak squeak' until the two needles on the indicator are depressed two-thirds down their scales. With forty degrees of flap and an airspeed of less than eighty miles an hour we glide in. I can see white cows in a field raising their heads from grazing as we approach, cottage washing lines in miniature, specks of white dust that are gulls following a plough. These things become less Lilliputian and more as we know them, houses are reality and people move again in the world. The pilot's eyes are unmoving ahead, his hands seeking the controls instinctively. We sink down over the road and the engines purr on, carrying us level across the field, barely over the hedgerow and then straight on to the beginning of the runway. Its near end broadens, rises and becomes hard ground rushing past. The engines barely murmur, but we still rest on the air with a soughing noise while the grass streams away on either side. As if playing a fish, the pilot eases the control column back and forth, feeling the aircraft's willingness to settle. At last it stays back against his stomach and our nose rises, but we still ride smoothly. At last comes the crunch of the first contact, we bounce a little and bump again, bump (pause) bump, bump bump bump — settling in quicker, harder bumps until we are 'all on the deck' and riding along gently bouncing like a 'bus with a carefree driver. We brake quickly, turn and charge across the wheel-scarred grass to dispersal-point where an erk scoops the air beckoningly with both arms. We come level with the other kites and stop. Soon the engines die out, props jerking stickily to a a standstill. The silence sings in our deafened ears.

* * * * *

I have read Masefield's *Land Workers* and thought it very good: perhaps in places it is a little simple or even trite in expression, as perhaps befits such an old man; but this does not occur often, and that very simplicity is more often an advantage, since it suits the subject-matter so well. Some of the poetry rolls off the tongue beautifully, the archaisms are charming and again apt, and at times I think the verse rises to a minor Shakespearean level, as in:

> Each year the blue September comes
> With wasps all sugar-drunk, in plums,
> And crackling partridge-stubble turned
> With trumpet-flowered bedëwind.

And the hull:

> Lurching like some ninth fatal wave
> That a mad moon's compelling drave.

And I like the final word on the 'quaint old country cottage' ...

> Whose leaky thatch was green with mould,
> Whose drink was from the brook beyond
> Or scoopings from the seepage pond.

Which is truth and not so picturesque.

And I have seen *In Which We Serve* a second time (from necessity, not from choice). The grand work by John Mills and Bernard Miles and the rest of them does a great deal for the film. There *are* some good touches in the dialogue, and at first it is all highly impressive, but the second time I saw it I realized the immense conceit of Coward written all over it. He seems to have built it around himself and he certainly gives himself a hero's part. I detect the preciousness in expression which I disliked so much in those short stories of his.

'Happy?'

'Ecstaticall-eh!' rolled off the tongue so quickly that it doesn't mean a thing.

*　*　*　*　*

12 February 1943

Flying is nearly all not-flying these days — one scrub after another, twenty-three hours is still the total. However, that includes my first night flight — three hours. If I hadn't by now forgotten all thoughts of danger (which at first I couldn't quite forget) I might have wondered how many minutes it would be before we hit something. I just couldn't see a thing. I had the feeling of being on the edge of the kerb in the black-out, at 120 m.p.h. We just fly on instruments and luckily it works out all right. There are two things in the world outside the cabin, which is nearly all shadow with a little dim light thrown across the instrument panel: a red light somewhere on the left, a green one somewhere on the right. In other words, our navigation lights on the wing-tips. Otherwise we might as well have our eyes shut − the darkness might be land, or sky, or cloud, there's no telling. Our existence is just one great big throbbing roar in a blank blackness.

Later I cocked my head up and was surprised to see wan stars, vague unearthly things which miraculously were grouped in a familiar way. So I was somewhere on earth after all.

We navigate by landmark and aerodrome beacons, each of which has a Morse characteristic by which we recognize our position. On a good night we can see them thirty miles away, and the solitary beacon to which we are heading is our one connection with the earth. A sort of star of hope, in fact. Everything depends on getting bearings from these and plotting running fixes.

Perhaps my description of the darkness is a little too sombre. I thoroughly enjoyed it all, especially as we got round nicely from one beacon to another (we call this a 'beacon stooge,' which is the easiest way to travel, but we won't be doing it again − in future we have to go from A to B regardless of beacons, merely getting bearings of them to check our position). The landing is the most thrilling bit. I have always felt about landing that a runway jumps from one world to another. By this I mean that it is always one of two things: a dwarf bit of track, quite impersonal beneath you as you circle, and when you touch down, miraculously broad about you, the grass rushing past, in fact just normal earthy surroundings. The transition period, during which you approach it and it broadens out, is a brief moment, and somehow you never see the ground cease to be ground-from-above and begin to be ground-around. You seem to be looking down on Lilliput at one moment, and the next you are in Brobdignag, with no idea how you got there.

The runway by night looks about as big as a matchbox, just a double row of fairy-lights somewhere beneath you in an engulfing darkness. How *can* you land on that thing? You can't tell whether it's a little thing a few feet beneath you or a big thing a few miles below. The engines cut out and you rush down towards it, jerkily aiming at it by quick corrections of controls, so that it swings about in front of the nose. Sometimes you see it above the nose or to one side, sometimes below, through the bomb-aimer's window. You make a mental note never again to say a pilot's is a stooge job. What judgment this requires!

The near-end spreads itself out a little, the engines come on and as you purr on to the runway a damned great searchlight thing comes to to give you your height judgment, and you touch down in its beam. And you BOUNCE, bounce, bounce, bounce-bounce-bounce-bounce ... like a coin spinning, that gradually settles flatter and flatter until it is all on the ground. The first bounce is a big one, and in between it and the second you are airborne again: then the bounces get harder, more frequent until you are rushing along quite smoothly like a 'bus, with those damned great lamps going past you on either side. You slow down and the engines rev. up alternately as you taxy round to Night Dispersal where an erk (another mental note; what a rotten job, and where would we be without them?) is represented by two waving green lamps, which seem to circle in a code understood by the pilot.

After the engines are switched off there is a moment of silence. The silence seems *very* silent, and nobody has anything to say. Then there are sounds of stretching and expelled breath, and we start to get out.

This is a grand moment. Nature's lavatory is by tradition by the tail of an aircraft, and while the pilot relieves himself you stand and look at the kite, which has assumed classic lines against the dark starry sky. So this thing has carried you safely all that way. And as it sits there on its wide legs, with the curve of the cabin top slanted up the sky, silent and with lights switched off, it's almost beautiful. A red light purrs slowly across the sky, and that's all there is that you can recognize about the similar machine which holds some of your friends.

Disillusionment now follows. You have to walk about two miles across the boggiest aerodrome in England, in darkness, and you fall into swamps and generally have a good time. But you can still stand and watch one of those red lights sinking towards you, silently, until the searchlight silvers the runway and a strange moth slides into its beam, a supreme reality which goes into the darkness again as the searchlight's job is done and it is switched off. Remotely another one circles in the sky above you. At no time have I found it harder to believe that those were noisy metal and fabric machines holding people well known to me.

The rest of the night-flight story is that we go down about 12.30 and were due to brief again at 1.30. That gave us six and a half hours' flying time in one night. And it was a pretty tiring business, because, apart from the dark and flying itself being somewhat tiring, navigation is an exacting task and when you fight the clock for three hours nonstop it requires a lot of nervous energy. We had to force ourselves to get into the air the second time. Luckily, however, I was first Nav. on the first trip, and on the second, my job being done, I relaxed considerably.

When we eventually got down I felt I could even do it again. (I must have reserves of energy somewhere because most of the blokes were staggering about half-asleep.) But as soon as I got into bed it was as if I was being chloroformed. I could *feel* myself being dragged into the realms of sleep faster than I have ever known it happen before. I only slept about six hours, and got up feeling tireder than when I got into bed. However, a good meal put that right and the Energy Altimeter is creeping up to normal now.

Plenty of fatigue, yes, but whether you're getting into a kite at midnight or getting your flying kit off just before dawn, when your mouth tastes like wet ashes and birdsong isn't even heard and a cock-crow is just a bore; or going to bed at breakfast-time and having breakfast at tea-time – the whole thing is clean out of the rut, you are living importantly. It's a real life instead of a suburban sham.

What a grand chance I have to see the Spring in.

AIRMAN'S WIFE

Carols a late thrush remindingly
But neither I nor twilight can turn you away.
So I watch you, and you watch aircraft on the rim
Of a green pool of sky, heavily one by one
Leave the just-twinkling flare-path, fierce with power
To surge black-bellied above us here
And sing away to darkness.

Though they have less humanity than stars,
The red remote lights circling while we pause,
That must not frighten you.

The faint cry of engines lost in night
Shall have no echo here. We young do not forget
Sunlight that ripples over the bright hours of day
Blessing our indivisibility. ...

But always, watching you, I understand
How much of life is evening, engine-sound
And being crucified alone at night.

(Spring 1943)

BLACKTHORN

They cannot have her for lover,
The lean brown southerly sprites
Who trade sweet breath for blossom
In star-pale April nights.

Though the cherry, Our Lady of Splendour,
Exquisitely fallen from grace,
Goes forth in white for their lover
In every woodland place;
And the wind-flirt apple, too eager
For innocence when they came,
Paints the dim skies of daybreak
With her gipsy buds of shame —

They cannot have her for lover,
The ice-white wanton sloe,
For she sells her kisses to winter
Whether they come or no.

(On leave, Spring 1943)

21 April 1943 (*to his brother David*)

This place is between Newcastle and Sunderland, in a miserable district of slight hills (hardly ever seen for haze) and an occasional slag-heap here and there. God, what a country. People live in stone hovels and talk what very nearly approaches a foreign language, and the towns are scored through by the wail of trams. I had a good look round Newcastle and I paid a lightning visit to Sunderland to-night, and there's not much to choose between them. However, most places are of interest in one way or another, and apart from the large rivers and ships and shipyards I hope to see a little of really slummish life around the back-streets, and see what it's like.

This is the real job at last and it's good to feel you're getting somewhere. We have met one or two of our old pals who got here a course or two ahead of us, now with brevets and stripes, and it's funny to think that in a month or so we, too, may have got to that stage. Everyone is worried a bit by the bogey of failure, more so than at other places, but we'll probably cope all right...

By the way, in case you're interested, I have appointed you my executor in my will: I hope you don't mind. I don't know what the hell it means, or what the job is, but you're the only person I could think of! Take a commission on it if you like. However, I don't intend to get killed. Just a routine precaution.

The 'drome itself is well run and we pupils have almost acquired some status as *nearly* air-crews. I went to draw my extra rations yesterday and find that a week's supply is:

3 eggs
3 tins of orange-juice
4 bars of chocolate
3 packets of sweets
4 packets of chewing-gum

and some vitamin pills. That is in addition to our ordinary sweet ration. One takes eggs to the YMCA to be cooked; last night I took my first one and had a smashing meal of fried egg, sausages, chips and coffee. That was the best canteen meal I've had in months. And in the ordinary cookhouse I've also had three eggs in four days, so there must be a surplus round here. The food is not too bad — I'm satisfied anyway. The main thing is to lower one's standard of expectation until all food seems tolerable, then it's O.K.

The brain-work during the day, though not exhausting, is not at all conducive to the poetic or literary state of mind. I'm now going to take another egg to the YMCA for supper. A wizard life!

*   *   *   *   *

(From a letter to his brother, May 1943)
We are flying and flying and flying. Every time I like it more. The most marvellous thing in this sodden, heathen country is to be able to go up *above* the clouds, forget about Co. Durham and play about in *real* sunshine. Some spirit of summer dwells up here, if nowhere else.

Yesterday we had to knock off work and come back early, and the chance to sit back and sightsee was rare and welcome. We chased another kite, out and around the clouds, which were those most beautiful things, huge white cumulus (cauliflower cloud). The sky was pure blue and when we turned one way the sun stared straight into my window like a great blinding thistledown ball. There was nothing but sun, sky and white cloud, and to play about in those conditions was sheer ecstasy. Poor old Brian is often sick and was shaken up badly by our manoeuvres, but I seem to be getting a cast-iron stomach and was as happy as a sandboy. It makes all the difference if you can take it.

(Early June 1943)
One bloke is breaking all the rules and regulations by keeping a fox-cub in the room. He found it in a snare just before he came here, and brought it with him: it dwells in a box with a broken bed over the top. Last night he had it in a sack, but the damned thing gnawed its way out and we had a fox-hunt at 3 a.m. A beautiful situation, because some blokes didn't know about it: wouldn't anyone think he was nuts if he woke up in the middle of the night to see a fox rushing round the room?

It's about two months old, about the size of a small fox terrier; a marvellous thing to watch, so very foxlike, with stone-grey, rather frightened eyes, and beautiful ears. It sounds rather stupid to say 'so very foxlike,' but after reading so much about them and getting rather a stereotyped idea of them it's quite a thrill to see the real thing in its full wildness.

* * * * *

Points to Recall (June 1943)
The cold, stark moonlight flooding the littered gardens in the winter nights after our bombing. 'The ice-dark blinding the eye and the bone,' the back-brain numbness, and the monotonous, clear owl-calls nearby around the gardens in their gloom-white serenity. The stars like diamond-points glittering with frost.

River twilight at Bedford. Terry and I took a boat out. Coming back, the water dim-sky-hued, glowing, and mist arising from the quicksilver surface like smoke. Too late perhaps for the summer ephemeridae and too civilized for the splash of fish. Border-river trees darkened almost to silhouette, the air fresh and still. And excellent companionship. Happiness.

It is a question only of developing the protective shock-absorbent layer over the nerve. For serenity, the nerve is rich with curd. When the latter wears thin, and the nerve itself is bared, we are like two men in a lighthouse where tolerance has ceased to exist; and nervous energy burns itself away like magnesium.

*   *   *   *   *

'He was twenty, a youth who swung ideals like sword-blades against the granite of his elders' thought. By its nature, the rock won: but he never gave up. He stood knee-deep in kindly condescension. He began to know that he was the untried, the defective in vision; no more than embryo humanity: a kind of mental leper to whom, however, time held out promise to cure.

Then one day in the summer of 1940 he outstepped them all by falling down the long sky in a mass of flame, dying. They had no answer to that.'

13 September 1943
My pilot is turning out well and (touch wood) it just goes to show that a chance pick-up can be a good one. He is a matey type, so my approach to him is not in the best Service tradition − I've never yet called him Sir, since it's so essential to be Gemini when on the job.

He had done two solo flights on Beaufighters, and after another one (which should bring him up to five hours) he is considered safe enough to be entrusted with my valuable life. I am keen to get on with it and have ceased to be prang-conscious so it's rather a bind having to wait. The first few flights will be really for his benefit and I shall have no work to do: and I am looking forward to sitting in the back of a Beaufighter with its magnificent visibility, and just sightseeing. Also to being able to go where we like, do as we please and have no instructor regulating our activities. And how nice it will be to evade the great disadvantage of Service flying − the necessity to work and thereby failing to appreciate the sensations of flying. In spite of my 104 hours

108

I never fail to get a kick out of watching cloud, the wing-tips, the ground and all the other phenomena.

12 August 1943
This morning we were out over the north edge of Cambridge. I had a look for what I could recognize. It was easiest to start from the river in the centre of the town and work outwards. First I saw the lawns and the Backs, so I went after a target I knew I couldn't miss, namely King's. I soon spotted this, looking a real monument, every bit as outstanding from the air as it is from the ground. Then I traced back along the street and was very pleased to recognize Caius. By now I had got the lay-out taped and I could see all Caius, with the square court-yard, even David's side of the square and the big main door: almost his room in fact. This was from about 3½ thou. It gave me a hell of a kick to think, 'Well, I've actually stood there.'

*   *   *   *   *

I want to get all available gen on civil airways. I have spent a lot of this war thinking of myself as a bloke without a foothold in any trade, and not much post-war future: but it has only just struck me that the RAF has been paying me to learn a fascinating trade in a growing business for about a year and a half. To develop this is the obvious course. I plan to write to several companies and dig myself in a bit. Since joining up I have realized what I denied at school – that I have *some* brain. Not an overlarge portion, but enough, and I'm damned if I'm going to throw away what I have on one of those office jobs in the Business World. I should be able to do better than that for myself.

*   *   *   *   *

15 September 1943
We are now at Coltishall, Norfolk. After a week I am quite favourably impressed. The grub (first consideration) is marvellous and the quarters comfortable. Otherwise it is rather an outpost of empire – but the advantage is that one must partake of exercise in order to get anywhere, which is a good thing. The whole trouble with this life is the lack of exercise. So walks and cycle wanderings, which are among the few

available amusements, bear double fruit. The country is well worth investigation.

A few evenings ago I went to discover Coltishall village. I cycled, and there was quite a thick mist reducing vis. to a hundred yards or so, which made things quite novel. On the way to the village I went along a completely deserted lane from which the country fell away a bit on either side: I ate many blackberries here. Then I came into the village and crossed over the river and then went along parallel to it. A few hundred yards along is a huge white-boarded mill where I watched several men fishing in the fast water below the sluice. The river looked picturesque with the mist and some glimmerings of light.

*   *   *   *   *

10 October 1943
Being orderly dog is not too bad on a Sunday – there are no rations to check in – but there are one or two binding jobs, the star-turn being the Lowering of the Flag at 6 p.m., at which I am to officiate and perform sundry embarrassing acts of blowing whistles, saluting, etc., in front of defaulters, S.P.s and other criminal types.

Later I have various duties, among which is contacting the WAAF Orderly Officer at a late hour and making sure that no WAAFS are in danger of having their Welfare shattered – the Decorum Patrol. More in my line!

Fred and I are practically 'There' now – we have one night trip to do. Already we are getting more regular days off, with the Flight, and it's nice to feel we are slipping into place.

Yesterday being our first pukka day-off we went to Norwich. A farmer gave us a lift in, and we returned by 'bus. It was nice to see some civilization – and it was Market Day into the bargain, which created interest and made the place crowded. But it is rather a dingy place. We ate, went to the flicks and ate again, and returned fairly early. We saw some auctioneering in the market – cattle, sheep, pigs, etc. Not an eventful day, but after this incarceration it sets one's mind back on the rails of a pleasant outlook.

Fred – my pilot – is an incorrible scrounger. He's one of those people who can't be anything but improvident. It's always 'Have you got any ...' and 'Can I borrow your ...' in a quite shameless manner.

110

As one of those who make it my business to be self-dependent, to look ahead and provide for my needs, I fail to understand how people can have so little conscience on these matters. Actually, without meaning any malice, I've learnt that forgetfulness and not having things are almost his strongest characteristics. Five days running he left his pump on his bike in the cycle shed, knowing it would be pinched, but just forgetting, each time, to take it in. Four of those five days he came out without his key in the mornings. He won't learn. Of course, the pump went. He has my pump, because it's less trouble than lending it to him several times a day. He has my valve rubber (the tyre leaked for a week, but received no conscious thought until it packed up altogether: then for the first time the lack is apparent – 'Where's Jim?'). Now I have no valve rubber in the repair outfit I keep in case my bike becomes unserviceable. To-morrow a parcel will go off to his wife sealed with my sealing-wax ... It happens several times a day. I'm just learning to be tolerant of it. Perhaps if he showed one whit of appreciation it would be simpler – but my help, my facilities are taken for granted.

The above is part of a character-study; not a tirade. Fred needs a lot of tolerance, and tolerance being like thin rubber with me it's the best thing in the world for me to learn to exercise it, to make it thick sorbo. He is a character built up of slowness, likeableness, goodwill and mental mediocrity: garrulous, careless in general yet thorough in particular; forgetful, improvident and unstricken by conscience as only these one-day Christians can be. I wouldn't change him. Through being as he is, he is doing me good. When I get annoyed with him I vow again to thicken the coating of shock-absorber over my nerves ... He talks a great deal, not very accurately: I learn to stand and let the flow of words wash over me without effect (it's no good trying to reply until the flood has abated). Occasionally I re-thread the needle of truth for him, with one word to his hundred. I am trying as always to see things truly. I think I am far more of an individual, more adult and more childish – adult in my incisiveness, childish in my perturbability – less worldly serene and having my own peculiar serenity when on my own.

*   *   *   *   *

111

We are not really needed here at the moment so apart from odd spots of aviation we stagnate on the camp. We don't get given official times off and we feel we want to be available whenever possible, so we don't get out of the place much. For the first few weeks, after a year and a half of vigorous training and/or mucking about, it strikes one as very pleasant to get up at eight, have no masters and very little work and adorn the ante-room for the majority of the time. But the sense of luxury soon wears off; for me at any rate, though not so much for my pilot Fred, who is thirty and appropriately more sluggish. We become like D. H. Lawrence's Kangaroos, fat-bellied, rooted to the earth by some powerful gravity, or however he puts it. The energy required to move is enormous. But mentally at least, my desire to return to the Northern Hemisphere and 'rush headlong at the horizon' is strong. I have views about mental and physical welfare, and activity is my favourite physic for both. I feel I would like a five-mile run every two days for a fortnight and then I could begin to call myself a decent human being. That's what I miss in this life compared with training. There is just no such thing as P.T. Now even at Brighton in the Black Period I was doing some wizard running and on the night following the Inter-Services Relay I felt fitter than I have ever done before or since. Flying and the exalted position of P/O are attained, but also disadvantages which I never dreamed of in my erk-days.

*　*　*　*　*

A few afternoons ago I disappeared on the Coltishall road and did about eight miles around the district, pausing to poke around a church and have two boiled eggs for tea at a pub and meander about the river; and my soul feels better for it.

*　*　*　*　*

We saw some quite pretty scenes over Norwich the other night, but nothing on the London scale. In a way I hope we get a bash when I'm on leave, because I have never heard or seen the post-blitz London barrage and from what I am told it's quite an experience. And professionally I want to see how things work.

*　*　*　*　*

Don has been killed.[1]

There isn't much to be said. I have no desire to graze the mere skin of the subject with a few totally inadequate words, and afterwards hate myself for the reduction of such complex feelings to a small and earthy medium. I am not going to churn out any of the routine clichés. To me it is as if one's feelings are a fantastic and elusive moth, and the effort to become articulate or to clarify is merely a candleflame raised to illuminate it, which instead sears its wings: and unwittingly destroys it. The act of doing that makes me despise myself for my limitations. So what there is, shall be unsaid.

The whole half of my childhood has been stripped away. Only a fool would be inclined at such times to start carving mountains with a penknife. But again what I feel is very little compared with the loss to his parents. I feel selfish in thinking of a loss to myself in view of that: all pity is needed by them.

The last being a miserably ordinary statement, I will stop before I make any more. I loathe the accepted trappings of death.

I have failed completely to express myself.

This life dulls one's awareness of tragedy. For about an hour after I got the news of Don it had me completely. I walked about heavy with feelings, as if in a trance. But the damned superficiality comes back on you, you've got to eat and talk and later fly, and it drives the deepness out of you. After landing I had to go back to where I left off. It's so difficult to think consecutively of anything wholly outside the normal run of life here. Only on my own is it possible. And by now, after a few days, the realization no longer strikes fully home at me. I feel ashamed at this, but I understand how it is. It's because of such things as happened a week ago, when I stood and watched a Beau fully loaded with H.E. cannon shells burning, knowing there were two people inside it. It was a fantastic and terrible sight, beside which a firework show is a mere candleflame. Yet I was no more than very slightly awed. This is the truth. Nobody was excited. Simply because it isn't policy. It's not a conscious effort to drug one's perception, but it's something spontaneous which comes with flying: the body protecting itself by a simple biological and psychological law. We just *don't* get tied up in knots by our imaginations, because it would then be impossible to fulfil our duties not only efficiently, but cheerfully.

[1] On 'Airborne Reconnaissance' in North Africa.

I know that to mention such episodes is not usual, but I have sufficient respect for Mother's mentality to believe that she knows that aeroplanes can crash and burn, and that awareness doesn't jeopardize my safety in the least. Often I wonder whether I am wrong and whether my enthusiastic straightforwardness which I take for granted also in her is tempered more than I think by the normal reactions of a mother. Cursed be the day when we two start kidding each other. I believe that she hasn't the common mental frailty of a woman, and that especially after her life, last war included, she makes good use of her sensibility rather than letting it run riot and become her master.

I never realized until now how much of my life included Don. The things I remember seem limitless. Our whole district is rich with memories of things we did together. For the first time I understand how much people − the spirit of them − can pervade places. These things I know I shall never forget as long as I live. The roots are too deep.

Possibly I shall visit Jean when I'm home: I must decide whether it will be any use or not. Poor kid: I remember when Mrs. P. told me Don had volunteered for airborne work overseas, I said, 'I suppose Jean's sorry.' 'No, she's very proud.' And I thought then (betraying my own youth) of youth's error: What if he's killed? I thought. But no, love and optimism possess the young heart, without that sanity-making pinch of clear seeing which would have made for balance in an emergency.

My religion has crystallized lately into a search for clarity. Nature helps me because I think truth lies there rather than in civilized mankind.

*　　*　　*　　*　　*

12 October 1943
Have just written the most difficult letter I've ever tried. Here is a copy:
　　Dear Mr. and Mrs. Powell,
　　I was deeply shocked to hear the news about Don, and I have been wondering since then whether I could say anything that would be of any comfort to you. In view of what I feel at the loss of my oldest and best friend, I can well understand what must be the extent of your sorrow; and there can be little consolation in the well-meaning words of others.
　　It is a platitude that words are inadequate at a time like this, and I have never realized until now the truth of it. My feelings are so

complex, my memories of childhood and youth with Don so rich, that it is futile to try and express them. In all sincerity I say that nobody in my life has had half his significance for me: he was as fine a friend for me as he was a son for you.

As you know, one's childhood in retrospect is a beautiful and nostalgic thing: and Don is an integral part of mine. The roots go too deep for me to forget.

These words are doing very little in the way of explanation, but I think you will understand how I feel. I would like to offer my deepest sympathy (in which my mother joins) to yourselves and Jean.

*   *   *   *   *

Sister Service

These three lie silent on the grass, since it is summer, waiting for their kite to come in. They have chosen a place several yards from the carpet of the blue-dimmed light falling from the rear of the crew-bus, so as to be away from the chatterers and the tea-drinkers.

Sex here has lost a little of its simplicity. These people wear stained trousers and grey low-necked jerseys with the sleeves rolled up. They know about the relief of strong language and the penetrative power of black grease. They know grudgingly about aircraft and enthusiastically about one another's private lives. They have quite tough minds.

Which is why I feel ashamed to have caught them in repose, back at their simple beginnings: broad-hipped and gentle-mouthed. Puckishly, one wonders how deep into the strange female heart this gum-chewing emancipation has gone.

Spread-eagled in the darkness, they look only tired, and as tired women do, a little pitiful: like dragonflies from whose wings the fire has gone. Their hair has met much slipstream since dusk and lies coiled and tangled about their heads on the grass. Their chins are thrown back in sleep.

We need a starter crew. Hating to do it, I waken one of them. Her eyes open blackly like a gipsy's, she jumps up. The lustre returns to the flaccid wing. Now, in the dim light, her breasts are deep-shadowed, her teeth gleaming. Suddenly feeling whole, I move away. Soon, as I stood beside the dark, huge shape of our aircraft, looking at the orange glow of the downward light on the grass beneath, and then at the white one above me, two of them bring the starter.

115

Their arms are brown, their hands oil-smeared, with black rims to the nails. They can look one in the eye and talk down to me about aero-engines. But they are women and the weight of the starter-battery makes them lean like beasts of burden.

I don't know whether to feel pity or pride.

(*Cranfield 1943*)

The Night Job

The flarepath in nights of summer is bright and steady, an avenue of escape across the flat mile of the aerodrome. It is our pathway to the sky.

Studding the darkness is a seeming riot of other lights, red, blue, white and green. Every light is the key to some activity. Torch beams swell up and down the humped backs and wings of otherwise invisible aircraft. Navigation lights, red and green, flash on and off, and downward recognition lights make orange pools on the grass beneath the aircrafts' bellies. Blue lamps circle to guide taxying aircraft. Torches shine on undercarriage locking pins, on bowser gauges, on pennies brought out to buy cups of tea.

Hour after hour the sounds of activity — shouts and laughter, the thud-thud of bowsers refuelling, clamber of boots over wing-roots — carry across the windless air: from first twilight until the dawn mist finds the aerodrome at last silent.

From time to time the eyes are dazzled by a glistening radiance which throws a white peace over the nocturnal scene. Every fuselage carries its distorted human shadow. In the background, hangars are caverns painted starkly with light and shade. Everything is revealed. There is the ground-crews' 'bus with several aircraft grouped about it in their expectant attitude. Towards it rushes a bowser loaded with whooping, overalled figures like holidaymakers on a harvest wagon. Ten feet in the air, a girl sits astride the nose of the nearest aircraft, one hand shading her eyes.

She is looking across the aerodrome, past the flood, at a solitary red light sinking towards us. It almost stops moving, glides a little to the right, grows in brilliance and darts smoothly into the beam whose glare hides it. As if by a supernatural transformation, no light emerges, but something incandescent with tiny, twin propeller-arcs, a shape delicately skimming just of the surface like a mayfly dropping its eggs

116

on water. Then the magic of the flood dies and only the red light, reappearing, remains. It slides across before us, rising and falling gently. It settles and slows. A ribbon of sparks streams away from an exhaust.

Night here wears a dress shimmering with jewels: jewels of varying voltage. And the old ones, the quiet stars luminous in the Milky Way – do they mock us?[1]

The patrols were long and towards the end became tedious. Unless one thought away into the mathematics of the business, there was no patrol. One does not fly to and fro at night. One hangs thunderously beneath a still dome of stars, always in the middle of a void, never moving. All life is suspended here in this vibrating shell holding its station in the dark. Ten minutes, and the same Polaris over the starboard engine, the same curved Plough drooping upon the wing. Looking back, one sees the same planet mounted like a navigation light at the top of the fin. Then a turn is given. Slowly one wing rises against the stars, and remains tilted. And slowly, slowly, those stars begin their procession past it. Greenish figures on the gyro slide round one after another, until the required one is reached, and with a slight lurch the wing sinks down, and we are level as before, but with a new set of sentinel stars gazing at us down the foreshortened top of the fuselage. Always we fly towards them, but nothing about them ever changes. The same sea waits beneath us. We are heading for Nowhere, and we never get any nearer.

Far away, back in the world, they sit in a shaded room watching a screen which sparkles regularly. We are a blob on the edge of the screen, lighting six times a minute, slowly fading, lighting again. The blob is moving. It is more ourselves than we are, because we hang motionless in space with our illusions of stillness and eternity.

* * * * *

I often think we have the easy end of this business. It was about a fortnight ago that I saw two of the pathfinders come in from Germany. The weather had made its big break about teatime – we saw it building up as we flew that afternoon: vast cumulo-nimbus hooded with cirrus leaning upwards from the north-west.

---

[1] Jim's first night patrol was on October 23 1943.

Dusk came half an hour earlier than usual, the sky above sombre with the massed cloud. After about an hour in dispersal we heard the rain begin to lash the roof as if a tap had been suddenly turned on. There wasn't even that breathless moment when a storm seems to pause to gather up its winds and fury. It just built up and up and let loose with no more ado. I looked out once to see cloud-gulfs blanched by lightning, like wounds in the heaving belly of the sky. The ground was half an inch under water, whipped by rain. Thunder boomed. Our aircraft nearby had strings of water guttering from the trailing edges. She stood as if unconcerned, but was soaked to the skin — or so one might say, imagining the dribblings into the cockpits.

When it had eased off I went out again to find blackness replaced by a revealing glare. The canopy was up. Four searchlights leaned inwards to hit cloud in a white mist of diffusion at about five hundred feet, lighting the whole countryside with their baffled glare. It was a cone with its apex amputated. The wastes of cloud were bluish, luminescent. Rain still fell lightly. And some poor devil are trying to come in in this. God knows how far he had battled through it already.

Yes, there was a red light streaking across below the cloud base, and the unmistakable throaty hum of a Mosquito. He went round several times. Under those conditions a circuit was practically the old joke of going round in a vertical blank with one wing on the perimeter track. I agreed with someone who joined me that 'he could have it.'

After the last circuit we couldn't hear him any more, so we knew he had gone out a bit to make his approach. He came in with one of those seemingly blind ugly rushes which are actually the best way out: with speed you can easily go round again.

We could hear him from a mile out coming in like the proverbial bat out of hell, straight and low and furious. It was the fastest landing I'd ever seen; or rather heard, because we followed his fortunes entirely by sound. He came nearer and nearer, and with a vicious rush was over the flarepath. He cut everything in a crackle of backfiring and went whistling and huming down the lighted lane as only a Mosquito can. You can't mistake the sound. There were one or two slight crunches as he touched, and a long soothing fall of sound which meant he was all on the ground and slowing. He took a long time to slow up. The sound faded into distance and we hoped not to hear anything else. We were all ready for the sound of breakages.

But soon came the calm revving up as he turned off the far end and we knew he had made it.

The second one came in about ten minutes later with identical tactics. There was something about their throttling back − the anxious note of the Merlins falling suddenly in a frenzy of barking reports and hissing away across the aerodrome − that fascinated me.

Meanwhile the old Beaus squatted stolid and safe around us, and we looked forward to another hour or two in the glow of the stove before supper. A grand life.

*   *   *   *   *

Now autumn is becoming winter and the aerodrome is a sodden mile of turf, the number of birds flocking to it is amazing. A few weeks ago it was gulls, but now these are comparatively rare and the stage is held by the plover. Vast companies of them wheel across the sky at dusk with their slow soft wingbeats. In the daytime there are thousands of them unseen out on the airfield. Their casualties from aircraft taking off are considerable. It is quite normal when just below flying speed to see them shearing away down-wind past the wing-tip, as if we were making a bow-wave of living birds as we rushed along. They are left behind whirling in masses like huge perplexed butterflies as we climb away. Miraculously most of them escape, but some are dashed to the ground in agonized attitudes, leaving often a fair-sized dent in the wing of the aircraft which hit them. In less strongly built aircraft they go right through the leading edge into the wing. I have seen an Oxford, whose leading-edges are wooden, carrying a crushed plover with its neck wedged into the broken plywood, and farther along the wing only a couple of large holes to indicate the complete penetration of some unfortunate birds to the inner regions of the aerofoil.

*   *   *   *   *

Heard from my Father recently … on how little he knows about what I do, how interested he is, etc. I replied I was sorry and then gave the complete low-down on security in no uncertain terms. He says, 'One reads so much about the activities of the RAF in the papers surely it wouldn't be giving anything away.' I can use my discretion about it when I see him personally, but I'm pretty careful in letters: of course, he feels 'out of things' − I would do in his position, with his RAF past − but it's just one of those things relatives have to put up with.

*   *   *   *   *

In Moreton Valence days there was a bloke we called 'Carpie' − a F/O with a moustache. He was the so-called dull boy of our course. He turned up here for a short time, and we've had a good chat about the old times. He has given me the low-down on why he never tried to work there, and in view of my present feeling about things it's reasonable. He surprised everyone by shining at the next place. I had rather got to like him towards the end of our time at M.V. and I now see he is a very decent type and has got his head screwed on far more soundly than we suspected. He told me that Walmesley was drowned. It seems his co-mate in exile, Dalton (the other Canadian sergeant), has also had it in some way or other. And so it goes on. A strange life!

A new experience on Thursday − the funeral of one of our boys, at which we turned out in full strength. My impressions are extensive, outstanding among them being doubt as to the necessity for the relatives to undergo so much in public. The mental torture in the mother was plain for all to see. I don't hold with all the procedure of funerals, but I'm very glad I went since my ignorance on the subject was profound.

Sand rattles upon a coffin. The little woman who will never now understand stirs as if to throw herself upon it: her other children hold her back, averting their heads. Only now out of this dream is the dumb grave, bordered by a stiff little line of officers: from the corners of their eyes they watch her, and in fascination she watches the coffin. Volleys startle the grey air. The womb dries up hard and empty, and in terror the little woman is whimpering.

*   *   *   *   *

An RAF Christmas approaches: we shall no doubt have a glittering twentieth-century celebration, but I'm not sure that it will be Christmas. I shall miss the institutions of carols from King's College on the radio (it'll be the same old jazz here) and the quiet spirit of the day. Whatever it means religiously, I love the idea of Christmas. It is semi-pagan

120

wonder breaking through the dull crust of our shifty-eyed civilization. It's the only time of year that I see people behaving with my idea of personal religion – joy, friendship, non-insularity. Everyone's perceptions seem slightly awakened. It's a beautiful time.

A few nights ago we had 20° of frost at only fifteen thousand feet. One kite was at twenty-two in 35° of frost.

Facing backwards in the famous Beaufighter near-hatch draught, I lost my right hand fairly soon. I haven't been so cold since early in 1940 on the farm at Epping. When I was at last able to turn round and begin thawing out, a strange thing occurred.

First I held my gloved hand under the heater – only for a short time, as I could feel the bursting sensation which indicates that external heat is not good when there's no circulation. Then I pulled off the leather gauntlet and the silk glove and rubbed my hand against the other glove. All things were now equal, though I didn't know it. My slight knowledge of physics supports it adequately, but at the same time I was slightly shaken to see greenish two-inch sparks coming from my fingertips when I began to push them into the silk glove again. Later I drew my fully gloved fingertips down the perspex and little bristly sparks, bright green, danced about them.

*　　*　　*　　*

Christmas Eve dawn, like a luminous mist creeping over the Dutch coast. A long patrol, cold, lonely, while the bombers go invisibly home beneath us, free at last from the sparkling flak that we watch to the east. Occasionally an amber-coloured flash, dying, which we cannot explain, or a string of red and green flares staining the darkness of Holland. We fly north, south, north, south until the last flak has gone up and the sea, coast and clouds are icily half-distinct in the sky-band of dawn.

*　　*　　*　　*　　*

First there is only the ghost. Far down in the black water, a ghost of light. It is a pallid thing, like a gleam on the side of some great fish that speeds through the depths. Very gradually it rises and gleams a drowned red, and then becomes brighter. And at last begins to writhe,

121

and is a dreadful orange fan racing across the water with a mist of the same light about it.

The blazing bomber sinks to embrace it. For a long moment, as if in a final agony, it holds off. But it droops. It begins to fly through a vaporous glow as the propellor-tips touch. Then the strength goes out of it, and four white ribbons sear across the face of the water, and very suddenly there is a great brow of spray flung forward, and a slowing surge, and the other bombers are going on alone while a flame dies into the sea far behind them.

*   *   *   *   *

The Norwich market-place at dusk on the same day, twinkling with the lights that will soon be out. Hubbub of last-minute shopping around the stalls, the real Christmas Eve spirit! Forgotten above, the sky droops dusky, the balloons turn and turn in secrecy. Down here a horse has slipped in the shafts of a hansom cab, and lies stiffly, steaming, the mouth agonized with exhaustion, amid a crowd of fascinated people. Suddenly compassionate, the man who has driven it all day looses the girths and harness, and his horror at this calamity is in his actions.

*   *   *   *   *

On Christmas Day we serve dinner to the airmen. The huge mess is packed, a dance band clashes happily, the noise is enormous. A magnificent meal is put forth. Serving is a blur of loaded plates, hands, faces, laughter behind which an hour and a half fly by, and suddenly it's all over and you realize you're one of the few 'waiters' left. So back to our mess for a scratch lunch. An auto-cycle purrs up and down the carpeted mess corridors, in and out of the ante-room, around the tables of the dining-room, amid immense merriment. It is ridden by a Spitfire C.O. who on dismounting creeps around flinging thunder-flash fireworks among unsuspecting groups. There is about ten seconds' delay while we scramble away from the hissing thing, then with a deafening crash off it goes and looses a wave of laughter.

In the afternoon the Christmas spirit manifests itself in Spitfires which fly across in front of the mess at 250 m.p.h. The best moment is when the kite turns towards you from a mile out, the nose goes down, it grows visibly, but without sound, then whoosh! it has streaked past in the hollow before the mess and is away up over the roofs in a steep climbing turn, already lost in the sky.

The Beaus perform too. They go over in pairs like sudden thunder, muted away abruptly in distance.

*   *   *   *   *

I've never had a better Christmas. The amount of bonhomie and glorious dissipation has (for me) never been surpassed. I got to bed at 3 a.m. after Christmas Day and 5 a.m. the next morning. It was a marvellous time, and we finished off the preceedings on Monday with more beat-ups. I was very pleased with Fred because he did a good one without doing anything silly – we used the method of the level, low approach across the 'drome at the objective, finding your height nicely before you reach it, then a pull up at the last moment. It's easily as thrilling and much more sensible than diving at the thing and pulling out violently, which usually results in some twit just pulling out too late and rather spoiling his future.

I'm getting a great deal of faith in old Fred as a pilot, whatever his failings as a human being. He took time to get confidence in the type of kite, but he definitely likes them, which is the big point. He's not a brilliant or outstanding flyer, but dead sound and competent. Which after all is the way to be if you want more out of life than a glittering and unfortunately curtailed youth.

Away from it
It is strange to lie once more at night in passivity 'under the aiming sky.' For three years it has been the lot of those about me to sprawl thus between their cool sheets, idly hearing the gruff thump of the guns and seeing the waxen fingers of searchlights blunted against the clouds of the far heaven: for to them it has always been this, the night beyond the window, remote, irrevocable in judgment.

Pressing my head back on the pillow, aware of the pallid familiarity of my room about me, I can recover something of that old attitude. I can delude myself into feeling that the star in the searchlight, moving and faintly murmurous, has never known our life. It has nothing in common with me, with humanity. It is part of the cold pattern of the night-sky.

123

Yet in the strangely poignant past of those newly on leave, the past of the other life twenty-four hours back, it was different. That star was our intimate concern. Waiting, our bodies yearned towards it. By argument and calculation would we make a stairway on which to scale the dark towards it, reducing it to metal and mathematics and finally to falling ash in our minds. Every movement was an advance, a potential menace to it. As we went out under the wings whose slant was into height and distance, behind the friendly din of our engines and the great propellers thrashing the air, we knew that the wastes of air were nothing. Only minutes were between us and our moving goal.

The night waited to embrace us, and took each of us in turn as a spent gust of wind and a dark shape snoring away to greater darkness; where we breathed and planned as before.

Within its steel husk moves the calculating seed of life. This is your height-lost star.

Gunfire shakes the windows with a sombre sound. The shells rush like hunting dogs baying into the distance. Then thump, thump, unutterably remote.

The hum of engines has died away. Quivering, the snow-light wanders on amid clouds in the black frame of my window.

It is strange to have no duty towards the sky.

*   *   *   *   *

I wonder how many civilians who thoughtlessly tune in at their leisure realize that it can be a bitter and disappointing pitched battle with Fate for some poor music-loving devils — such as myself. So far out of five Delius Week programmes I have heard one, but I hope to hear tomorrow's. On the first morning I put 7.15 on the door and to my intense chagrin the batwoman turned up at about 9.30. On the second morning I was in bed at dispersal, but had asked one of the erks to wake me at 7.15. The message went astray during the night and at 8 a.m. I woke up having had no call. On the third morning, determined to hear *Over the Hills and Far Away*, which contains one of the loveliest passages in all music, I had prepared soundly by chalking up 7.15 on the early call board — this always works — we use it when we come on leave. During the night I am told it was seen to have become 8.15 and by the morning had disappeared altogether. I woke up at five to eight in a state of extreme madness. The thought of those twenty-five minutes of delicious pleasure which had slipped past my innocently sleeping head each time made me wonder if any effort was worth while. On the fourth morning I actually got a call at the right time and listened in to *Appalachia, Sea Drift* and the Bissell gathering up fag-ends with much scrupeting off the ante-room floor. On the fifth morning I got to bed at 1.30 after five hours' flying during the day and night, and said 'Hang it.' I slept comfortably until 10.

I hope to hear *Paris* to-morrow. I have one chance in ten. Or should I say a hundred? But I *did* hear the Violin Concerto on Wednesday, in spite of the row in the ante-room. So I can't grouse.

* * * * *

Golden mornings of boyhood in the Flying Field, in summer. Tall grasses, four-foot wild-parsley massed on the skyline, over which float our slow models, dove-white, bearing a thistle-wheel of sunlight in the propellor's arc. June zephyr in which they hang, drifting over against the distant-green woodland mass, stationary, falling, sliding into hiding in the grasses. Joy as we run to fetch them where they cant steeply among clover and poppy, energy spent. Knowledge of our surroundings when re-winding: cuckoo flying over, calling; butterflies white and brimstone and red-velvet drifting from flower to bright flower, the summer-morning space-murmur, faint voices of children playing by the far hedge.

Don and I always experimenting, flying by rule of thumb, ignorant of finer points, laughter-making. David often apart, a head and shoulders on the skyline, calculating, watching his model soar like a gull over our sparrows.

And ever the real flyers, the larks, singing into the height of the sky.

* * * * *

PALE BLUE WINDOWS

Warmth and discreet light lave the corridor. It is carpeted, dome-roofed in polished woods of exotic origin, the walls intricate with studs and switches. There are windows, functionless and curtained with heavy blue stuff, for it is night and nobody here has need of the stars. Down both sides twinned armchairs like vast purple sundews secrete the bodies of the travellers, drawing them down into hollows of exquisite repose. From these lips of peace spill only an occasional arm or leg as label to what lies within.

Some of the pilgrims – business men – have switched off and pushed away their reading lamps, and sprawl flattened beneath their own bellies beyond whose oceanic heave sinuate the almost naked dancers on the television screen. These are happy men: whole men, because they are invariably the richer by these last twelve hours and on the strength of this their stomachs have been recently and sumptuously filled. They are within two hundred miles of home. Everything is to hand. Why not, then, be happy? With the bright eyes of lizards they follow the interweavings of the dancers. Catspaws of pleasure cross their damp flesh.

For nothing need the arm be more than half-raised. Here in the silky curve of the wall are mounted the lamp-switch and the filter-selector: tinted lighting caters for every neurosis. Beside them the tray from which by an ingenious device, ready-lighted cigarettes may be drawn. Watchfully the reading lamp leans down, moon-faced at the end of its pliable giraffe-neck. There is a general cabin heating, but to ensure the comfort of the old and very successful, whose blood creeps stonily about the body, there is a puce-coloured plate, a magnificent radiator by every lamp. The extent of its benediction is governed by a rheostat control knob. Many are turned fully on.

Finally, of course, set into the arm of every other chair, there are the television selectors; ten buttons, worn smooth by the fingertips of many pilgrims searching the ether for scenes of ever more charming voluptuousness. The sets are back to back on a common table, each facing a pair of the thick purple seats, whose occupants must needs have common tastes. Mutual lack of taste satisfies the requirement, so that the arrangement is invariably successful.

A wave of the hand brings the steward and a six-page menu. Orders are given quietly since there is little noise. Once accustomed to the rumour of smooth power, one can be unaware of motion; except when drinking. The liquid in a glass is dead level, but occasionally scored by a tremor of hairlike lines across its surface. Thus far are we still imperfect.

There comes a stiff, young-old man in flawless uniform, white and gold. He is older than his hair, which is dark and bears his cap as at the crest of a wave, crazily, about to topple. His face has lines of exasperation and humour, neither of which is yet master; but they are in great strength, and have been fighting it out for a long time. Straight down the corridor he walks, gravely as a man who is past life. He regards his two prim feet preceding him along the carpet strip; between the rows of televiewers tuned to one frequency like dogs' noses to a tree, past the waking and the sleeping who are identical, away from the amber pools of light and the debris of limbs and the neat black paunches and the floury bosoms. To the other end.

He has looked to neither side. There is nothing here for him. A door opens and closes gently and he is gone.

He stands behind the two pilots and sighs. It is refreshingly cooler out here, and the engines more audible. All darkness leans thickly inward against a core of light, a rosy glow over the instrument panel, against which are silhouetted the bodies of the pilots, slumped back with folded arms. Their heads are above it and are vague, blocking out stars.

The nose is strutless, of moulded perspex, so that one seems to be standing unprotected on a dais beyond which is all the vast powdering of summer stars, close enough to be touched. Below is a void. But far ahead there appears to be a radiance as of glow-worms scattered, faintly luminous after death: the lights of land.

His vision continues to improve. First the thick darkness, then the stars and the cold glimmering ahead. Now he looks to either side thoughtfully. There is something for him here. The wings and engines, like the heads of the pilots, are merely blotting-out of stars. Not one engine a side any more, but six. Each a forward-thrusting shape beautifully slim, with a steady bar of blue flame riveted to its flank. The perspective tremendous to the wing-tip; six masses of engine over-lapped, foreshortened. And beyond the wing-tip, the stars beginning.

They have their machine, steady as a rock, and their solitary light; and now after these hours, the delusion of man in the air that he is unbound from the earth, and the universe wheels about him.

Thompson, the first pilot, sighs too, wondering that after twenty years of this he should see things with so much newness. But then he is on his last flight, and at such times everything hitherto unseen rises up, to be gleaned painstakingly against the future of looking back at faded reflections in mirrors. Thompson is greying. His time is running out. Never to see the thing itself again is not good. So, wide-eyed, he gleans.

The smooth shape behind him fidgets and swears. Thompson looks back, stretching himself.

'What's new, Mick?' he asks, speaking professionally.

'Nothing,' replies the wireless operator. 'Now or ever,' he adds as an afterthought.

'Why the vehement language?'

'Oh, a bit browned off. Any coffee there? – I've had all mine.'

'Yes, some. But not very warm. I should get some from the steward.'

'So-and-so the steward,' remarks Mick cheerfully. The slanging reminds him of the old times, which they share. This is better. He takes the dark cylinder that Thompson proffers and begins unscrewing the top.

The second pilot, plump and youthful, wakes and looks round.

'Hullo, Tod,' Mick greets him. 'Having a rough time of it?'

'So-so,' says the youth thickly.

'Tough.'

Mick drinks. His eyes gleam balefully in the reddish light as he leans forward between them. 'Eleven-thirty, eh? Twenty-five minutes to go. Hundred and sixty miles. Makes you think, Tommy.'

Viciously he screws on the bakelite cap.

'That's all right,' murmurs the younger pilot before Thompson can reply. 'That's progress.'

Thompson, after his forced jocularity, has sunk back into his mood of taking all and giving nothing. He will not reply now. 'Progress,' he turns the word over and over, savouring it, thinking heavily of his twenty years and what he has seen come to pass.

But Mick wields a knife-blade of a voice. 'Progress. Oh, yes.' He is becoming characteristically dangerous. Thrusting back the thermos, he looks away from those two bulky shadows to that other blackness, the wing heavy with streamlined cowlings and its tip steady against the stars.

'Progress,' he begins slowly. 'We're doing well. Smooth. Straight and level. Hardly a sound. And they sleep.'

'Who?' asks Tod.

'Back there.' His voice gathers impetus and becomes icy. What he calls Back There is something he will never let himself forget. 'They

128

sleep, blast them. Heaps of old washing. Walruses. Harlots. And the comfort! Man, they couldn't have felt cosier on their wedding nights.'

It's true, thinks Thompson, true. This much I've seen come to pass. 'You see, they are rotten with it,' says Mick. 'Just look at them. Are they flying? Do they know? They might be under the sea for all they care. How high are they? Are they still in your hands or have you two baled out and left them to it? Are they going where they think they're going? Ask them. They don't know.'

'And why should they?' comes a tired voice from the black hulk that is Tod. 'It's all automatic anyway.' He has heard all this before and has little time for it.

Thompson nods sadly, affirmatively. With his heavy judgment he tries to seal the matter. 'It is. We are. Everything is. I hate it as much as you do, Mick. Have done for years. I'd give anything for a few manoeuvres, a bit of real flying. But we're on rails now and we might as well get used to it. It's not the same any more. That's all.'

Tod tears things open again. 'Nothing's on rails,' he argues. 'What about taking off and landing? You don't do a straight-line circuit, do you?'

'No,' concedes Thompson, 'but that's different. Even nowadays a circle has to be round. Still, I daresay that'll be put right in time.' The sands are running out fast, and with them his patience. He has all those other things to put away, how it is with one's head against the stars, the feeling of throbbing suspension in a waste without movement in any direction – yet measuring by those land lights we have moved and are nearer the end; the very slight pulse of the metal one touches, weaker than blood or anything human, but alive; the look of those torches of constancy, the exhaust flames, which have companioned man ever since he first flew at night. All this must be saved, not some third-rate argument.

Mick is unshakable. He leans forward, his face underlit with the ruddy glow so that he is like the others, a grave gnome with a roseate chin, sunken eyes and no top to his head. Fervently he speaks to Thompson. 'Back there, back of beyond, I like to think how it would be if you shook those bastards up. Pull her up and over in a stall turn, you know, Tommy, and then away down for all she is worth. Straighten her into a screaming dive. Let the speed and the pressure build up until you feel as if you're going through bloody concrete. Your artificial horizon there, with the datum line stuffed at the bottom of the picture. Then bring the line back to the little dicky-bird by a long pull and a strong pull that will push those Back There knee-high to a duck on the floor. Drowning in spilt whisky. Oh boy!'

Thompson, now only half preoccupied with his stars, feels his hands twitch a little with the fascination of it. It would need so little power; the idea, his own many times before, can still bewitch him. But to-night his mood takes in the end of all things: he is sunk in dreadful finality.

'Mick,' he says, 'we aren't so young any more. We'd probably find we couldn't take it either.' It is a strange job, he decides, where you finish up old and then go back into a world which gives you thirty or forty more years to live. But the only conceivable world is this one – flying – and you're through with it. Those temperatures. ...

He runs a careful eye over his instruments. He looks ahead at the remote, steady lights of the city, crowned with a bluish five-thousand-foot haze. He looks upward at the stars, which are cold and unmoving. But this time he does not hunch back into reverie. The germ of older days has got into him after all; and absently he begins to reminisce.

'I used to get a kick out of the scrambles at night. You're losing money fast at pontoon and a few minutes later listening to the roar of her guts as she pulls you off the runway. Those last few lights sliding away beneath, crinkly because you're looking obliquely through perspex, and then you're on your own.'

He pauses over some private memory, and putting it away again, goes on.

'Throttling back, your mind as clear as a whistle. Pontoon? Never heard of it. After an hour or so you were bloody cold and cheesed and beginning to think back to card-tables again. But the first few minutes were 100 per cent. good, because you'd done away with little things that really didn't matter. Stakes were big and nobody but you could do anything about it. That gave you a feeling you never get nowadays.'

Mick moves, the better to see him. He faces straight ahead, his eyes shadow-filled. Does he see everything or nothing? The voice becomes sing-song with melancholy.

'Now we've landing and taking-off devices subsidiary to a mechanism that never eats or thinks or sleeps, but takes us a thousand miles in a dead straight line and keeps all those needles steadier than if they were painted on.'

Thompson gazes at the approaching lights. Beyond the massed radiance of the city, now flickering with nearness, he can see a little pool of amber in which floats, becalmed, the tiny strip of runway. He switches off the automatic pilot and takes the control column with his left hand while with his right he eases back the linked banks of the throttles. Momentarily, sound dies. The lights rise before the nose. In gentle magnificence the machine rests on air, now with a soothing, singing note. The city opens out beneath it, and streams away behind. There are lights on every side, multiplied over the polished skin of wings and engines. Blazing reflections slide away down the nacelles, succeeded by more and more, ever clearer and more numerous as the height decreases. Thompson crouches with his eyes half-shut, like a cat in the sun. He is scared of himself.

'I met a man,' remarks Mick dreamily, 'in one of those kites. A veritable mountain of pork. "My man," says he, "can you conduct me to the lapis lazuli inlaid convenience?" "No," says I, "hold it until you get down like we used to, and then stand by the machine and let it go on the grass. It makes the ground feel better. You can hear your engines clicking as they cool. You can see the dirty great shape of what's just brought you through several hundred miles of sky. That's the good way."'

'And when Company heard?' asks Tod unkindly.

'Oh, I woke up selling bootlaces to my old woman. Well, I'll tell them we're in the home stretch. So long.'

The door closes behind him.

With exquisite ease Thompson banks over into the circuit.

Now it is all done with for the last time, he can chuckle at the thought of the grave Mick pacing away towards his cabin through Back There, with an expression of frozen superiority, looking to neither side because he is of another age and another Service and his nature is not pliable: so that there is nothing here for him.

Those who know only the Master Thompson, with his calm and detachment, cannot understand why the lights of the machine, as it murmurs a mile out on one of the flawless Thompson approaches, suddenly bounce upwards and there flowers the roar of full throttle on all engines. Incomprehensible to the whole aerodrome staff is the subsequent behaviour of that machine: it seems to hang in the sky, growing at an alarming rate with a swelling of engines, and with a mammoth snarl

131

has shot overhead and is away, two lights level, now tilted, now standing one above the other in the darkness. There are cries of shame and mortification from the officials now crowding to the windows of the vast reception buildings. Thompson is on a VERTICAL BANK.

Light and sound fade. There is a fevered buzz of voices, bells ring, women scream and even faint. After some minutes of hubbub everyone becomes quiet again save the sobbing women. They await the return.

Their attentiveness is rewarded. Now they can hear him coming in, straight and level and low, and flat out. He comes from the direction of the city, whose roofs he is reviewing at fifty feet. For a moment his lights seem not to move. With a howl they take a dislike to each other and fly apart. Now between them swells the mass of aircraft, overhead and gone, and the furrow or vacuum behind it fills up with a sound of slithering air, like the lash of an invisible tail.

It has lasted no time, and is over like a dream. The boy whimpers at his side, but unheeding Thompson holds her straightly into the glide. He has seen the face of Mick twice; first with puzzled joy as he returned at the opening of the throttles; and then afterwards at the last steep turn in, when the wireless operator returned from Back There with an expression of radiant exaltation which bespoke the answering of all his dreams and prayers. The age-old battle of his face was won in that moment.

It was bad and it was good. The sudden fire had gone through him and out of his hands, away into the machine and out to earth somewhere, he is left brittle, dry and empty, but complete.

They will be waiting down there, with oaths and threats and perhaps policemen. The ambulance will be waiting for the outraged ruins of Back There. But all that matters is to keep thus in the smooth murmuring glide, with those tamed gleams caressing the nacelles, the short patch of darkness beneath and then the widening mouth of the runway, the peacehaven streaming away on either side, the calm playing of the central column and the kindly prolonged crunch as she settles.

*   *   *   *   *

Fred arrived back looking more married than ever, and definitely more married than aeronautical.

132

I suppose I'm sometimes hard on Fred. Sometimes it's justified and sometimes I'm just a bit cheesed. Admittedly he has the roots: I consider it often and I realize that I don't appreciate all the difference it makes however hard I try: for anyone in the single irresponsible state it can't be fully appreciated. But I do maintain that nobody with such roots should come lightly into a job like this: once in, the decision made, one's duty should be to the job. After all, it's voluntary. Ideally speaking one should be able to give oneself fully to it or not to undertake it at all. No slight on Fred, of course.

Never for a single moment have I regretted the day I joined up. That's a permanent satisfaction which can override the temporary and trivial chafings of any way of life. That is how I would have it; and yet, I've felt ashamed all the way along to be living this pampered and comparatively safe life since Don's death. And when some of the types show the usual lack of enthusiasm for any sort of effort, I feel, 'Oh Christ, it's little enough we have to do; what sort of stature could we have in the eyes of the dead?' I begin to appreciate what must have been the original excellence of the now hackneyed term 'supreme sacrifice.' This may all seem a little histrionic, but it's as honest and spontaneous as anything I ever felt.

To-day a whole gang of us went to one of the beaches, the best I've seen yet. The sands round here beat any of boyhood's holiday haunts hollow, and when you throw in the good old West Country rock coast, slopes of dazzling gorse and an inconceivable brilliance of sunlight out of a clear blue sky. ...

*   *   *   *   *

Spring Returning, 1944
The fine spell began with a morning of sunlight slanting out of a liquid sky where cumulus was already forming. At the eastern side of the fields were long shadow-islands of wet grass. Swallows swooped and beat to and fro before the house, burnish-breasted in the flowing light.

As the sun arched higher the light became crystal-hard. At midday the sky was studded with piled cumulus whose tops rose snowy and clear as scrolled marble against the blueness of infinity. The atmosphere was clean-washed, vigorous. Vast fretted shadows trailed over the rusty wastes of commonland with its gorse like splashes of molten gold, and through the powdered green of copses and over the brightness of the meadows. The air was drenched now with sunlight pouring in columns between the clouds, and somewhere beneath their bases, which were grey and yet glowing, the light-filled shadow of the Impressionists, floated the songs of innumerable unseen skylarks.

Along the brooksides and at meadow-fringes, by paths of hardened mud, shone celandines an inch across, and, in the same star-form, but pale, anemones too fragile to look up into the sun. Duskier, half-unseen in the richness of grass, were many bluebells. The home cattle, leaving the harsh meadow light for the incipient summer-shade of trees, pressed through this wave of flowers to the brook, where they stood with lowered heads searching the water, dipping and gulping with ripple of pendant neck.

By evening they were back at grazing: gnats formed knotty vapours over the deserted brook, drifting and swaying. The water was lower now, and ran without sand. A golden light lay horizontally over the land, and taking their mood from it a thousand blackbirds and thrushes carolled peace. Flattened rags of clouds dissolved into the sky-lake of dusk.

Light died westward, leaving the world a pool of shadow startled by desperate thrushes. A curlew flew the length of the glen, trilling beads of notes that hardened into a few glowing jewels and slowed to silence. Now from the lawn field I could see a band of smoky orange light on the western horizon, against which lay jet black the skyline of the aerodrome: long flat hangars, the small citadel of the control tower, a mast with a drooping windsock: the insect-shapes of aircraft. To the left the distant hills were hard and blue. All the fields about gleamed luminous with afterglow.

I went and sat on the terrace of the house which all day had been standing blind and white above its starry meadows. Now everything was drowned in dusk. Before me floated the glimmering shapes of the cattle, deep black and ghostly piebald; the red cows were like poppies seen in darkness, blood-gleaming. The bulk of the bodies was just felt: there were no legs; the cattle drifted as loosed shapes in the field, uncannily. But they had their labels of sound: the clank of wire rubbed by an itching hide, and occasionally the deep husk of cattle that is like the stroke of a handsaw biting into oakwood.

On the second day no cloud appeared. The sky was dried out. Now there was only brilliance which deepened blue as it became hotter. A faint purple-greyish line of haze lay about the horizon. The anti-cyclone had set in, giving air stable and empty save for this hard edge of haze which from above would have a pearly opaqueness towards the sun.

All day the cuckoo called, and the herd strayed glossy-flanked in bright worlds of grass about the house, or pondered in the thick shade of its sheltering chestnuts. When I climbed the field after lunch the grass rose glassy-green to the intolerable blue of the sky against which the cattle lay: placid shapes half-silhouetted; black, creamy and darkly glossy like a new-peeled chestnut.

The lake was like quicksilver among its massed trees. White blossom clouded the quivering water at the far end. Here and there were the pink rhododendron flowers, the first from bushes which between them held tens of thousands of fisted buds, fresh green, tightly folded, promising huge banks of fire-blossom for the summer, lighting the water.

First darkness that night was creamed by a dying new moon. A faint mistiness lay among the trees. From where I stood outside dispersal I could hear curlew-song drooping away over the aerodrome, disembodied in the dark. When the curlews were quiet again a nightjar came and hawked up and down across the bracken waste: or so I knew by the short whirring calls which came like the work of a ventriloquist, now near, now far. I never saw the bird. It had a definite hundred-yard beat, but it was impossible to say from which part the call would come next.

When I climbed the lawn field at midnight the white rim of moon had set. The house stood pallid among a dark softness of trees. It was dead calm. The Milky Way glimmered like a river in mist, flowing between Night's meadows many-eyed with star-flowers.

In the afternoon we flew towards North Devon — Lundy, a scar in the haze, floating in distant sea-sky: to our left the coast, cloven by the gleaming wishbone-shapes of the Two Rivers. Lundy Island grew clearer, and the Island Race was beneath us in the sun, blue water woven with brown stains of recent floods, issuing from the river estuary.

Our nose lay over the island. Lundy gained detail, opening like a flower before us. Not the barren bird-haunted rock of my imagination, but tamed into the patterns of agriculture, with here and there a cluster of farm buildings among the quilted fields. At the south end, perched on a line of rocks like bird-droppings, is the lighthouse − the wan light whose flashings swelled and faded through Atlantic vapours to that headland watcher of twenty years ago. The light then was almost lost in distance, the island beyond a half-thought; now I could span my fingers over the lighthouse and the headland and the sea between, and without memory there would be no magic in this country which lay in simplicity about us.

But it had not changed. To a watcher on that coast now we were only a thread woven into the fabric of a spring day: a remote speck murmuring away towards the sun. For him there would be the old bird-song, the bright flames of the gorse, the hushing of the sea far below. Then again would come the throb of our engines from the heights of the sky as we came eastward again. The land was as rich as ever. We were the exiles.

We turned three miles off Appledore. These mottled wastes of sand with the ivory smoothness of the tideline were Braunton Burrows. They seem plain and very limited. But of them Williamson wrote, 'All sense of time and place is lost, and a man becomes a spirit of sea and air and sky, feeling the everlastingness of life while larks sing shrilly overhead and the bones and skulls of rabbits lying in the desert are of a glowing whiteness of eternity.' Here below us were a couple of miles of greyish sand − all spirit of place is lost from the air.

We were too high to see the white specks of gulls gliding past the headland (those specks with still-held wings which shoot past like rockets at lower altitudes). But they will have been there, jostling into the red furrows inland where the ploughman barked at his team. Everything down there was tiny, smooth, unpeopled: lanes like hairs, villages a few grains of brown earth among the red and green squares of their fields. Here in these few miles of bland countryside lay buried a million words. I thought of the travail of the one man who formed them: would his bitterness have embraced us, looking for one minute into his life through the wrong end of a telescope, ignorantly?

*   *   *   *   *

24 June 1944
'Incidents' occurring. Hence our sudden presence here at Audley End, on Midsummer Eve.

The country is totally different: smooth, just-undulating land, golden with hay, green-dusky with corn; marvellous trees and lawns around our billet, a 'rambling old place' at an unspeakable distance from the scene of operations, the most important of which is, of course, eating. However, we manage. The place has the most fascinating outhouses, lofty barns in the best Cambridgeshire tradition, beautifully built, but now somewhat decayed by time into dusty granaries cluttered up with ancient implements and acroon with pout-breasted doves which nest high up in the rafters. For a person with a curious mind and a sense of the past it's a treasure-trove.

Farther afield there is my favourite town, Cambridge. I'm looking forward to one or two very pleasant days there if spare time permits in this latest piece of gipsy life. What a vast experience this all is!

*   *   *   *   *

I must admit I am a willing pupil in the arts of the Simple Life right now; circumstances are happily accepted. There is a certain virtue in saving money, reading good books and gazing out on the countryside with a pleasantly torpid mind, and with the help of several runs round the neighbourhood on off-days I'm even succeeding in feeling fit and pleased with life.

I went to Newmarket Races with some of the types, and had a wizard time watching the life that crawls and stalks around such places: bet only once and lost 10s.

Two visits to Cambridge have been distinguished by a studious doing of the wrong things: the price of going out with well-meaning types with not much width of vision. Having seen the streets and the pubs they pronounce Cambridge just a very ordinary town: not a glimmer of the Colleges, the Backs, the University Library, and so on, has ever crossed their consciousness. Admittedly the virgin town Cambridge has been transformed into a third-rate prostitute by the war: the place is filthy with Yanks and their various trappings, and the former scene of part-culture and part-good and merry life is now a hard brassy pleasure-seeking ground. Everything is cheap except the food and drink.

I must say the old characteristics still peep out: I've seen some lovely popsies of a most blood-stirring kind, but even these show signs of being American-trained. We'll have to get the mob out afterwards, quieten the streets down a bit, raise a lot of values and then Cambridge will resume its position with me as the most pleasant town it's been my privilege to know.

I was home on a forty-eight and saw a lot of doodle-bugs (wretched name!). On the second afternoon I was at the Oaks Corner during a walk and a goodly bunch came over in about five minutes. One fell about 150 yards from me. Loud bang, punch of blast, huge mushrooms of smoke, stink of explosives, shower of drifting leaves, but no harm done. So far nothing has been too near the house − touch wood. A good sprinkling all over the neighbourhood, but the nearest to us when I left was about half a mile. Mother remarkably cheerful: a very brave, sensible type. Can't think of any more at the moment. There's a most God-awful row on the wireless which hardly permits thought.

(*Coltishall 1944*)

* * * * *

The Dream

Several of us were advancing from post to post, mopping up as we went. The enemy, in twos and threes, had dug in every few yards. Our infiltration from the rear was entirely successful. They appeared not to notice us as we crept up and destroyed them with grenades or revolver fire. We were in the open, and sometimes attacked individual emplacements from the flank: and though we kept as low as possible it seemed altogether too amazing that we were not seen.

After several such minor victories we found ourselves at the rear of the house. This also was vulnerable. Entering without opposition, we went forward to a room with an open door, through which several of the enemy could be seen clustered about the window with their backs to us, firing intently: and as with their comrades, so these were completely unaware of our presence.

I do not remember seeing any of them specifically. They had no characteristics of build or dress, nor was I aware of their nationality. They might have been men or women, and I did not know how many of them there were. One merely felt them as a power of danger. The Enemy.

We considered blasting them out with a grenade as they stood. I had a long handled pineapple grenade in my right hand, of a type I had

138

not seen before. It was studded with short black horns like a mine. How has it to be fused? I turned it over and over in my hand, finding the protuberances all alike and equally meaningless. Merely throwing it would probably not detonate it. I could not use this thing.

We came to some decision, and leaving my comrades to carry out the final attack, I went silently back and made a wide arc to cover the front of the house. No more shots came from the dark window-space. I found myself in the open, standing up to watch. Although the enemy was still within, and unliquidated, I felt no danger. Something was distracting their attention, and I had every confidence that shortly they would have no nerves to startle nor eyes to frame me in their sights.

In that moment our attack must have taken place. I think there was an explosion. I am not sure. Almost immediately someone had climbed through the window and was standing against the wall of the house looking at me. She was young and dark, and unarmed, but I knew with a prickly feeling of fear that she was The Enemy. I looked down at the grenade which was still in my hand, desiring now more than ever to know its secret. My confidence had gone. This girl alone was nothing, but I had no idea what still waited behind the blank gap of the windows, menacing me. If she had survived there might be others.

There was no sense to be got from this outcast of grenades. I slung the wretched thing away behind me. With the sudden movement there was a tightening against my waist – the revolver belt. Feeling that I had turned from darkness on to a straight clear road flooded with sunlight, I pulled out the gun and broke open the ammunition pouch by the holster. The shells, I remembered, were in a crumpled matchbox. Would one have escaped, to be loose and readily attainable in the pouch, or would I have to fumble away valuable seconds bursting open the box? My luck was in, there were several loose rounds. In inexplicable optimism I only took one. Everything now went with soothing simplicity: the breaking out of the chamber, pushing the one shell home. As always with my own revolver the chamber jammed open a little, but I flicked it home hard, and found myself with the cocked gun levelled at the girl who was slowly coming towards me. Still nothing had happened to me. I began to feel a little better.

All I remember about her face was its equanimity. There was no anger, no terror, no hatred, no intent of any sort. I know she was dark and vaguely beautiful (her beauty was a sensed quality, I was concentrating not on her, but on her significance; the potential menace which might even now lie behind her: I had no concern with how her beauty was made).

At last I realized two things simultaneously. That she was harmless – there could no longer be anything left on the other side of the window – but that she was The Enemy, and valueless. She was only here to be destroyed. And I found myself knowing already that I was going to destroy her comfortably and easily.

She came unhurriedly, and I waited serenely, remembering the short effective range of the revolver, and holding my fire. She could have broken away suddenly, and I could have wasted my one shell after her, and there would have been no ending. But she showed no sign of fear or realization. She just came on. I watched her in happy fascination.

I saw afterwards that she was wearing trousers the colour of sand, and a white shirt, but at this time there was no detail at all except the quiet face and the mass of dark hair. Her face was like a spirit gliding into my ken.

She was near enough for me now. Her calm could only have been matched by mine: I floated effortlessly in a still pool of well-being. My hand holding the revolver was steady. This was The Enemy, and a worthless life. I shall never forget the ease of sighting the revolver at her breast, and firing.

She had fallen. At once I was off again towards the house. I remember distinctly, as I passed her, the red flower that had grown through the white cotton shirt, a little below the heart and to the right.

In the house I ascertained that our work was done. There was to be no more resistance. I left my comrades, feeling a change in myself. Now the taut pleasure of the battle was over, I felt the wind blowing from another quarter, and I took to it as easily. I had forsaken that other road, and was now unconcernedly embarking upon this. It was not disquieting; although what had grown into me was pity.

As I went outside I looked at my revolver, and put it away, closing the flap of the holster. That was at an end. I went back to the girl, who lay twenty paces from the window. With surprise I saw that she was breathing. Into the quiet waters of my pity flowed hope, and I felt a certain tenderness for her. I raised her to a sitting position. The shirt clung to her by the red stain, as if pinned to the flesh: looking more carefully at the position of the wound, I saw that it was clear of the

140

heart, and I began that the bullet had lodged in the central juncture of the ribs. I supported her shoulders and placed my left arm under her knees. She was light and easy to lift. Here she was no foe, no shielder of menace, no gliding face, but earthly, sweetly made woman as I carried her away.

In spite of this I at no time felt shame at what I had done. We had all striven in battle, my comrades and I, to eliminate these people rather than be eliminated. She had been of this enemy, and indeed was to me The Enemy itself, as every individual is in opposition. When the gun is levelled there is no Enemy save this one in the sights, and this is The Enemy complete. I had done my duty, and having subsequently been victorious and able to afford pity, would try to save her. That my victor's pity included a personal tenderness was something to which I could not admit. If the others saw me with this enemy there would be no ignominy for her − we were self-disciplined − but I would have to lay her down and some man murmuring the names of his lost family would gently shoot her through the head. Afterwards I would have to be careful, for my tenacity of faith would be doubted.

We were not seen. Somehow there was no more fighting anywhere and we had come to a hospital where I took her into a ward and put her down on a high padded bench just inside the door.

'We will leave her so,' said the white-smocked doctor, who had appeared immediately without any sign of surprise at what he saw. 'No, we will turn her round, this way, and she can stay here until we are ready.' I lifted her again and placed her more comfortably across the bench, with her feet on another placed at right angles, touching it. As I settled her head she opened her eyes and looked at me with recognition, but no bitterness. Neither she nor the doctor had behaved as if anything abnormal was happening: they might have been playing over something already well rehearsed.

A little later I came back and saw her still there, but fully conscious now, with her legs drawn up under her, leaning back and watching me calmly.

What I did after that, away from the hospital, is not clear. I was back again the next morning, enquiring (shamefully, for I knew no name) for 'Yesterday's casualty.' They had no news for me. She was not in the ward. I went away and came back later, asking again for 'the girl who was shot' and wondering what the hospital staff would think if I were to add that I shot her. The third time I had a feeling she was dead. After great delay they told me she was alive, but in great pain, her stomach and liver having been partly shattered by the low-velocity bullet. She would live, but she would never be whole and healthy. The stomach would give trouble. No, I could not see her.

(AT THIS STAGE I WAS HALF-AWAKENED BY AIRCRAFT ENGINES, BUT LAY WILLING MYSELF BACK INTO THE DREAM, TO FIND THE ENDING. I MANAGED TO PROJECT MYSELF BACK, TO PAY ONE OR TWO MORE FRUITLESS VISITS TO THE HOSPITAL, DURING WHICH THE REMARKABLE CLARITY OF THE EARLIER EPISODES DECAYED INTO THE FAMILIAR DREAM-ENDING OF A SENSE OF FAILURE TO RECAPTURE PAST EVENTS AND TO FIND AGAIN THE PERSON WHO HAD COLOURED THEM FOR ME.)

Notes

1. All movements simple and unrestricted, none of the familiar 'heavy-as-lead' strivings of many dreams. Details remarkably clear, especially with regard to my revolver, the bullets in the matchbox in the left-hand pouch, the tendency they have to escape loose into the pouch, and the temporary jamming of the chamber which is peculiar to my revolver alone.

2. Calmly waiting to shoot, with one round, easily tied up with poaching expedition when I waited minutes for an approaching rustle in corn to come near enough, saw at last dark shape (hedgehog, it afterwards seemed) sighted and fired my one round (and missed!).

3. On review, with little anatomical knowledge, damage to liver seemed impossible from bullet in lower ribs. But on checking with M.O., found it quite feasible. I HAD NO KNOWLEDGE OF THIS WHEN AWAKE, BUT MANAGED TO FIND CORRECT DETAILS IN DREAM ALTHOUGH I DIDN'T BELIEVE IT AT THE TIME.

* * * * *

AFTER NIGHT OFFENSIVE

Glowed through the violet petal of the sky
Like a death's-head the calm summer moon
And all the distance echoed with owl-cry.

Hissing the white waves of grass unsealed
Peer of moon on metal, hidden men,
As the wind foamed deeply through the field.

Rooted to soil, remote and faint as stars,
Looking to neither side, they lay all night
Sunken in the murmurous seas of grass.

No flare burned upwards: never sound was shed
But lulling cries of owls beyond the world
As wind and moon played softly with the dead.